It's Going to
Sting Me!

RONALD ROOD

It's Going to Sting Me!

WITH ILLUSTRATIONS BY
CARRYE E. SCHENK

DISCARD

McGRAW-HILL BOOK COMPANY
New York St. Louis San Francisco Bogotá Düsseldorf
Madrid Mexico Montreal Panama Paris São Paulo
Tokyo Toronto

PRINTED BY ARRANGEMENT WITH SIMON AND SCHUSTER

FIRST MCGRAW-HILL PAPERBACK EDITION, 1977

2 3 4 5 6 7 8 9 0 MU MU 7 8 3 2 1 0 9 8

LIBRARY OF CONGRESS CATALOGING IN PUBLICATION DATA
ROOD, RONALD N
    IT'S GOING TO STING ME!
    INCLUDES INDEX.
    1. DANGEROUS ANIMALS—UNITED STATES.
I. SCHENK, CARRYE E.   II.   TITLE.
[QL100.R66 1977]   591.6′5′0973   77 7203
ISBN 0—07—053579—5

To Charles Weigold,
to whom no plant or animal holds any fear,
as he loves them all

Contents

O Lord, how manifold are thy works! In wisdom hast thou made them all: the earth is full of thy riches.

—Psalms 104 : 24

1·Ghoulies and Ghosties...

Somebody was following me. I was sure of it. I could hear soft footsteps, back there in the dark.

I glanced around at the silent Vermont woodland. The lights of our house were a quarter mile away; there was no nearer human habitation. The snow around me, falling in huge sticky flakes muffled every sound. Trees were bowed with its weight; snow-burdened bushes and evergreens looked like grotesque figures—silent, watchful.

No car could be expected along that gravel road. Even the snowplow had made but a single pass, much earlier in the day, so the surface was covered by several inches of new, clingy snow. Little could be heard beyond the soft pad-pad-pad of my boots as I strode toward home at the end of an evening walk.

It was shortly after our house lights became visible far ahead that I got the feeling I was not alone. It took a while for me to become aware of them, but then I heard them plainly: footsteps in back of me.

Some other traveler was abroad, I told myself; doubtless one of my backwoods neighbors. I stopped to wait for him.

When I stopped, however, he stopped, too. No sound did he make; he just stood there somewhere in the dark. Well, if he didn't wish to walk with me, that was his privilege. I turned homeward once more.

Instantly he started up again. I could hear him back there in the gloom, his footsteps almost exactly in time with my own, but a fraction of a second later: pad (thump), pad (thump), pad (thump). He neither came closer nor dropped farther back—just kept pace with me.

I went a few more yards, then stopped, one foot raised in midstep. Sure enough, I had halted so abruptly that he'd been caught off guard. He hadn't stopped as quickly as I had, and there was one more footstep: *thump!*

An odd sensation, like prickly heat, flooded over me. Who was behind me anyway? What did he want?

Then I heard a voice—and it was my own. "Hello!" I cried. "Who's there?"

No reply.

"Hello?" I ventured again. Still no answer.

This was no friendly backwoods neighbor. Should I retrace my steps and try to see him, or should I continue on toward our kitchen light winking far down the road?

The kitchen won out. That dark tunnel through the woods behind me had nothing to commend it at all. Besides, I reasoned, if Whoever-it-was continued following, maybe I could at least see him in silhouette when we got down near the light.

Then, from a snow-laden evergreen along the road, came the answer to it all. Unable to bear the weight of its load further, a branch dropped its heavy burden to the ground. The snow hit the slush beneath with a *thump*—and there was the clue to my unseen pursuer.

As I'd been walking, each footstep had picked up a load

of sticky snow. Clinging to my boot a moment, it had dropped off as my foot went forward for another step. My silent companion had merely been clods of snow falling in perfect timing, naturally, with my stride.

The extra step? Simple. It had been the last lump of snow, hanging for a moment as my foot stopped in midair, then dropping to earth with that final thump.

That unsettling little event took place years ago. Since then I've had a number of equally unnerving experiences in the pursuit of an outdoor life. I've been followed by wildcats, divebombed by owls, cussed out by raccoons as if they were about to eat me alive. Once, as I lay curled in my sleeping bag in a remote portion of the Adirondacks, I was awakened by a gentle tapping on my derriere, as if some creature were stealthily feeling out the best place for an attack. I've heard groans and yowls, sighings and breathings—all startling, but all explainable.

More later about these and other delights from my years in the wild. Right now it is *you* who are in jeopardy. There you are—under the scrutiny of a buzzing hornet, say, or the uneasy center of a ring of glittering eyes out there beyond the light of your camp fire. How will you survive the next ten pounding heartbeats? What can save you?

Well, this book can—in a way. Not that it will quiet all your fears, or even attempt to. A little tingle of fear is a wholesome and healthful thing, and a safeguard against a multitude of woes. I remember learning, back in my days in the air force, that there were *old* pilots and there were *bold* pilots, but never any *old bold* pilots. Those goosebumps that warn you not to go beyond your depth or your understanding, as it were, are a good safety device and well worth heeding.

On the other hand, the panic that may occasionally

threaten us all seldom produces any good. I have seen people speechless, unable to move when confronted by a mouse. An insect flew through the car window of a friend of mine. In his frenzy to get rid of the offending critter he ran off the road and totaled his automobile—although, luckily, he injured nothing more personal than his dignity. And a visiting little brown bat emptied the dining hall of a boys' camp right in the middle of a songfest.

It is true that there are creatures out there that can harm you. They can even do you in under certain conditions. Snakes *can* bite, bees can sting, spiders can put you in the hospital. Nor does this book pretend they cannot. It's the unreasoning fear, grown out of proportion—the fear that can spoil your fun and make you miserable—that should yield to a little of the treatment set forth in these pages.

After all, had it not been for the snow falling off that evergreen at the right moment, my leisurely stroll might well have collapsed into headlong flight down the spooky road, pursued by little clods of snow in double time. That's what the Unknown can do to you.

So, better to meet these purveyors of panic, animate and inanimate, right in their own haunts, whether said haunts be a lonely cabin in the forest or merely a tree-shaded picnic table near a hamburger stand. Bravely armed with your guide and dutifully following its illustrations, you should be able to face that summer vacation, that overnight hike, that picnic in the country, with something less than acute apprehension.

Herein you'll find explanations for (and pictures of) many of the things that screech and creep and bite and sting—or at least look as if they might. Once the Unknown is known, and has taken on personality and character, it becomes less threatening. Then, perhaps, you may not only get out in the country, but you might get down to earth as well.

Indeed, it's possible that you just might even survive.

2 · ...And Long-legged Beasties

When I left you, a page or so ago, you were staring apprehensively at a hovering hornet. You're on a Sunday picnic, perhaps, or you're harvesting a crop of wild fruit you spied from the car. The hornet, apparently, wants to harvest it, too. On the other hand, you may merely be in your backyard minding your own business. A single hornet can put an end to the whole affair.

Before you abdicate, however, and leave the field to that meddlesome midget, here's a brief word about why it's there. Once you understand the ways of hornets you're better equipped to cope with them—and even escape their unwelcome attention.

Have you noticed, for instance, that when there are hornets around there may be few, if any flies? This does not always hold true, as there seems to be an endless supply of flies. But, given a little time, a nest of hornets will get rid of most of the flies in the immediate area. If they only had keener vision, they'd be dreadful flytraps, indeed. However, hornets are woefully nearsighted—at least from our standpoint. I have seen these insects cruising along the side of a building, just a few inches away from its weathered clapboards, alighting on every knot and nailhead with a purposeful little pounce. Occasionally the "knot" would turn out to be what they were seeking, and the hapless fly would be seized, stung, and borne away to the nest.

Many farmers know this redeeming detail in the lives of hornets. It is common to see a cow grazing in a meadow, attended by her usual retinue of flies—which, in turn, are systematically preyed upon by half a dozen hornets. The flies, chewed to a pulp, are fed to the grublike hornet larvae in the nest, while the adults themselves feed on the juices produced in the pulping process. Thus hornets reverse the usual food role between adult and young: the juveniles feed on solid food, while the grownups imbibe the liquids.

So, a grudging Score One for the hornets: more hornets, less flies. However, since they are attracted by sweets and the juices of fruits, these stocky members of the wasp family may be so persistent that you'd rather have the flies. Then, too, if you accidentally squeeze a hornet, you're bound to get much the same treatment accorded its other victims. Is there any way you can persuade it to allow you a peaceful coexistence?

Happily, yes—or at least partly so. A little foresight helps here. The sense of smell of most insects is far keener than our own. Male moths have been known to fly more than a mile in response to the come-hither scent of the female. If you're on a picnic, keep those aromatic peaches, those tempting pears under wraps until you're ready for dessert. Keep other fragrant food covered, as well. If you're out in the hammock in the backyard, dispose of empty beverage cans and similar attractive items. And forget your he-man after-shave or sexy perfumes. They may attract more than the opposite gender.

At the other extreme, there are plenty of good insect lotions on the market. Eating garlic helps too—really. Or try a little camp-fire smoke; it's a good repellent. If the insects stage an invasion, arrange your seating so an occasional wisp of smoke blows your way. It may sting your eyes a bit, but it's better than some other stings you might otherwise collect.

If you're a smoker, save a puff or two for the insects. Not that you should blow a cloud right at a curious hornet; you might confuse it so that it'd zero in on your nose. However, very few insects can stand the smell of tobacco— except a few aberrant critters such as some ants who seek out the filter tips of discarded cigarettes and drag them back to their homes. With our growing emphasis on the outdoor life, and with our North American population out among the insects more and more, I can see the cigarette ads a few months hence: "Proven definitely 43% more irritating—to hornets, mosquitoes and bees."

Bees, by the way, are generally more tractable than their cousins, the hornets and wasps (technically, "hornets" are social wasps, such as the whitefaced hornet and the yellow jacket, that live in colonies). A honeybee is slow to use its weapon; the reverse barbs on its tip prevent the sting from being withdrawn after use. Thus a honeybee must pull away, or be brushed aside, leaving the sting partially embedded in its victim—a loss that is fatal to the bee.

Usually you can avoid being stung simply by keeping calm. But if you are stung by a honeybee, do not remove the offending sting with fingers or blunt tweezers. You'll merely squeeze the poison sacs at its base, thereby injecting more venom. Better to flick the sting away with a fingernail or knife blade, and thus avoid an unscheduled booster shot in the arm.

There are some bees that do not have any sting at all. Such a situation is scarcely as idyllic as it may seem, however. These insects, mostly native to the tropics, are quite capable of defending themselves and their homes. If an intruder threatens, they attack in a phalanx of jaws and claws, squirting an irritant body secretion into the bites and scratches which they inflict. The sensation is about like wearing your long-handled woolies on the Fourth of July —only worse.

There is another kind of stingless bee—and wasp, and hornet, for that matter. Up to this point I have avoided referring to the sex of these insects, but here it is: the ones that sting are all females. They have got to be. That lethal sting is, in reality, a modified egglaying apparatus —and that, of course, lets the males out of it completely.

Many people have heard of drone bees, those creatures that do little work around the hive and exist merely to impregnate a new queen on her maiden flight. Drones look like the worker females, but are slightly larger. Their heads seem to be almost completely helmeted with huge, compound eyes: perhaps the better to see and follow the virgin queen several hundred feet into the air. Once she has mated with a single drone, the queen returns to earth —leaving scores of suitors unfulfilled.

Fewer people know that there are drone wasps—and hornets, too. They also resemble an outsized worker, often with impressive optical equipment. Like its drone cousins, each exists in the slim chance that it will be the one to mate with a newly formed queen.

Since none of these drones can sting, it would be convenient to be able to pick them out from among the other insect visitors, and thus spare yourself some unnecessary jitters. However, such is seldom the case, as you must have all three types to compare: queen, drone and worker. Of course there is one sure-fire way to tell the difference—if given the chance, does it sting?

Even here you may be fooled, as drones often buzz and hum angrily when molested, and even probe around with that stingless tail section as if they were about to deliver a hefty wallop. Since the sting of many insects contains formic acid, that final proof of performance might well be called the acid test.

There is one type of drone, however, that can readily be distinguished from his fearsome mate. This is one of the most familiar wasps of the northern United States and southern Canada: *Polistes*, the common house wasp. They're shaped like their sisters, but colored differently; instead of being a general chocolate brown like the females of this northern temperate species, the males are liberally splashed with yellow. Yellow faces, yellow legs, yellow rings encircling their bodies lend a two-tone effect.

Polistes builds an open paper nest in attics and under eaves; the nest looks like a tiny umbrella hanging down from a slender tip. During the summer the house wasp slowly builds up its colony to several dozen individuals. Its increase takes place at the expense of thousands of flies, gnats and mosquitoes—accompanied by misgivings of the farm wife over whose door they have taken residence, even if she knows house wasps for the peaceful, helpful creatures they are.

All summer the burgeoning nest comprises an aggregation of Amazons, who feed and care for the youngsters. Then, in late summer a generation of drones is produced. The males buzz around the outside of buildings by the dozens in the September sun, awaiting the new-fledged females. Often in an apparent case of mistaken identity, one male will suddenly clasp another—only to be set straight by the recipient of such attention.

Eventually the new reigning female mates and flies away to seek a hiding place for the winter. The males continue to play in the sun, while their paper home, now neglected by the workers, no longer produces any young. One day a killer frost hits them. Only the new-mated queen escapes, safe beneath the bark of a tree, or hidden in an attic. She alone lives through the cold to start another colony the following spring.

Those exuberant males are common on the insides of windows during the golden days of early autumn. One impressive event of my college days was when our zoology professor, Dr. Russell DeCoursey, sauntered over to several wasps buzzing at the window, inspected them briefly —and calmly picked up a male in each hand. It was a lesson in applied entomology that I never forgot. I have since done it myself in the classroom: it sure gets the attention of the students.

Incidentally, if you try this stunt, be sure you're dealing with the bona fide northern *Polistes* male. There are plenty of other two-colored wasps around, all primed to deal with any undue familiarity. But if you see a yellow-banded wasp consorting with a chocolate-colored one, you've got the right species. Once you've identified it in this way, you can spot it every time.

There are *wingless* wasps as well as stingless wasps. You have probably seen one of these creatures if you've poked around under stones and boards as a kid: it is commonly known as a velvet ant. Covered with a short, fuzzy coat, the velvet ant is blatantly colored a bright red or orange. Handle it and you're sorry at once; the mohair-clad creature lives its life on a perpetual short fuse, weapon always at the ready.

I remember one occasion when our entomology class was collecting insects in the field and a member of the group found an attractive velvet ant, nearly an inch long. He reached down in spite of the instructor's hasty warning, picked up the ant—and flung it away instantly.

"Gotcha, didn't it?" said the instructor.

"Nope," said the student, unwilling to admit to such a rash performance. "It just doesn't take me very long to look at one."

Although the velvet ant is really an earthbound wasp, there are some genuine ants that give you the same treatment if you play fast and loose with their nests or protesting little persons. The notorious fire ant of our southern states is so gifted—with the delightful little habit of hanging on with its jaws while it delivers its sting. Such behavior recalls a Canada goose who once attacked me after I had blundered onto her nest: she hung on with her beak while she thrashed me with her wings.

There are many other members of this quick-tempered family. Many can sting, after a fashion, with that pointed egg-laying apparatus, or ovipositor. They range from great ichneumon wasps with trailing, threadlike drills four inches long to tiny winged insects who could fit comfortably on the period at the end of this sentence. Between them are creatures with delightful names like horntails, sawflies and tarantula hawks.

Horntails are harmless but fierce-looking, with cylindri-

Ichneumon Wasp

cal body and a quarter-inch spike that brings up the rear. The spike is not a sting, however; it's part of an apparatus for penetrating the trunk of a tree, laying an egg, and thus launching a wood borer on its devastating career.

The ichneumon, in her turn, uses that long drill to tap down to the borer's tunnel and lay an egg of her own. This egg hatches into a predaceous little larva—and soon there's no more wood borer.

Sawflies actually cut away at plant tissue with a blade-like "saw" on their tail section. The tarantula hawk is a huge wasp that catches and paralyzes large spiders as food for her young. To round out the total, there are some hundred thousand other species known to science in this great group, called the Hymenoptera. They range from wasps who lay eggs in the bodies of aphids—or plant lice —to bees who live as uninvited freeloaders in the hives of other bees.

All in all, it's quite an assemblage. Looking back over the list I've compiled it occurs that I may have made it *too* complete. Perhaps, after reading this far, you'll resolve never to go out into the awful outdoors again—like the medical student who, when he'd heard all about man's dreadful diseases, decided to live on nothing but boiled milk. However, let's assume you have braved the wilds, and are back where this chapter started—only now you have dutifully spirited away from your victim the fruit, the empty containers and other aromatic niceties. Yet here she comes: a non-drone, unexpurgated female of questionable temperament, giving you that withering Once-Over. What do you do now—show her this book where it says everything will be all right?

Hardly. But there are a couple of things you do *not* do. Don't wave those arms; the myopic creature might interpret your antics as a threat. And it is neither wise nor dignified to run; a kamikaze hornet can outsprint a horse.

The best action is almost no action at all. Remember the insect's poor eyesight: if you remain motionless you'll merely resemble a blob on the landscape, even if the creature lands on you. Shut your eyes a bit; if the curious insect sees its reflection it may come closer for a disconcerting better look. If you can slowly get any material between you and your airborne guest—a napkin, a handkerchief, a leafy branch—you may divert its attention while you gracefully make your getaway.

Suppose, however, that the Ultimate happens. Assume that your contrary little companion doesn't know how she's expected to act. Perhaps you and she wanted the same spot on the chair—and you learned of her intentions too late. Or possibly you impulsively brushed her away—and got pained for your pains.

Score Two for the little lady. She got a bull's-eye, there: a direct hit with a pair of fiery needles. But unless you're one of the unfortunates who may suffer from envenomization—allergy to the sting—it'll all be only a painful memory in a day or so.

Envenomization in a small number of us is a medical problem calling for instant professional aid. But there's help for the rest of us, too. One of the quickest sources of relief is most likely right at your feet. Common mud—either the genuine stuff from a handy pond, or a hasty patty made with moisture and a bit of soil—cools the white hot down to boiling. Or make a thick paste of ordinary baking soda and water and spread it on your outraged epidermis. A dab of household ammonia on the spot helps, too.

An ice cube gently rubbed around the edge of the area will also ease the pain and swelling. Rubbing it right on that peppery little pimple may help as well—although you'll half expect the ice cube to burst into steam.

It's scarcely surprising that the Hymenopterans have a number of imitators among the other insects, with such a potent device for keeping enemies at bay. Certain flies and moths, for instance, are shaped like a bee or wasp. They buzz like one and even twist and bend as if to sting like one. Until you've learned to recognize these impostors they may give you many an anxious moment.

Sometimes you practically have to be a bee or wasp

yourself to tell the real from the fake. Since the world of the birds and bees is liberally sprinkled with these copycats, however, we should take time for a couple of clues as to their identity.

The most commonly seen impersonators are found among the flies. One species, sometimes called the bumblebee robber fly, looks surprisingly like its black-and-yellow namesake. It's portly and fuzzy like a bumblebee, and even lurks around flowers in the garden. It's there on a more surreptitious errand than the peaceful bee, however, for it captures and eats other insects—including the bumblebee itself. It's completely harmless to humans, by the way, in spite of its awesome colors and proportions.

There are several flies that you'd swear to be honeybees, too, until you were enlightened. They're known as drone flies, bee flies and flower flies. They also linger around blossoms—sometimes in great numbers on asters and goldenrods, drinking nectar just like those hardworking "white man's flies," as the Indians first called the honeybee. There are also wasp flies and hornet flies—each one with a shape and color so like that of some Hymenopteran that it can wander through life undisturbed by all sorts of troubles.

And how do you, glancing uneasily at a dozen insects on your marigolds, tell whether you should wade fearlessly among the flowers—or decide that you really didn't want a fresh-picked bouquet, anyway?

Nothing to it, if you can count to four. The Hymenopterans, it seems, have four wings—or none at all, in the case of ants and their allies—while flies never have more than two. Once you've counted the wings, you've got the answer.

If you have the heart for such things, sneak up on a

Robber Fly

Bumblebee

questionable character with a wide-mouthed jar and cover. Gently surround it with the jar and clap the cover in place —including the blossom, if necessary. Explain to your family what you're doing as you consign the captive to the refrigerator for fifteen minutes to quiet it down. Then inspect the wings with a magnifying glass. If it has but two wings, no matter how fearsome and ill-tempered it may seem, it is only a fly.

Behind each of the two wings of a fly, by the way, is a tiny knobbed structure on a short stem—the halter, or balancer. In some mysterious way, these two balancers are vital to flight. If even one is injured, the fly performs barrel rolls and goes into a tailspin. If both are injured, it spends the rest of its life walking—or buzzing helplessly on its back.

One word of caution, however. The fore and hind wings of many bees and wasps are often fastened together with a series of little hooks, like a zipper. Thus they, too, may look like only a single pair of wings. But each wing arises from a separate point, so look at their bases to get your total number. This, I suppose, is sort of like counting the legs of a crowded herd of sheep and dividing by four to find how many individuals are in the flock. However, it's well worth the effort, especially if your mystery guest is present in the fields and meadows by the hundreds—as often happens during early autumn when insect populations are at their exuberant height.

Even a moth may fool you. A number of them bear a startling resemblance to wasps. Like the wasps, they have four wings or none. These mimics have long, slender wings, appropriately zippered together, and may even be colored brown and yellow, like a regulation wasp. Pick one of them up and it may actually prod you with its abdomen, as if to sting.

Hummingbird Clearwing Moth

One look-alike, the hummingbird clearwing moth, is as large as a hummingbird. It boldly visits flowers like some sort of great robust wasp. However, with your handy jar, refrigerator and magnifier, you can penetrate any moth's disguise.

Wasps have sturdy jaws that work from side to side for munching on insects, ripe apples or even wood fibers to be chewed into paper for their nests. Moths possess a long tube, coiled like a watch spring beneath the head until extended for use. So if you see the "watch spring," no jaws, and a hint of the fuzziness typical of its kind, you're in the presence of a moth. In spite of its alarming appearance, it can do you no more harm than a butterfly; indeed, for practical purposes, a moth is just a first cousin to a butterfly that looks as if it needed to go on a diet.

Besides the stings and the mock stings, there is the world of charming denizens of your beach party, your lawn siesta or your after-dark affair—the gnats and mosquitoes. Your magnifying glass will confirm it, if you have this device along on such occasions: gnats and mosquitoes are in reality specialized flies. They have the two wings and the pair of halteres possessed by the rest of their tribe.

Together with the horseflies, deerflies and greenheaded flies, these creatures cause about as much misery as all the other insects combined. Not only do mosquitoes transmit such dread plagues as malaria and yellow fever, but the African tsetse fly carries tropical sleeping sickness—in addition to the pain of its own bite. Add to these the trouble caused by black flies, plus the unwelcome attention of the tiny no-see-ums or punkies who may hide beneath your wristwatch strap, under a tight-fitting collar or in the brushland of your eyebrows while they perpetrate their deeds, and you've got quite an assembly

Biologists, duly impressed with the qualifications of these small attention-getters, have awarded them scientific names that hint of their ability to get mixed up where they do not belong. Among the mosquitoes you can find such epithets as *Aedes vexans, Theobaldia impatiens,* and *Mansonia perturbans.* An unwelcome guest in the cow pasture is a small fly dubbed *Lyperosia irritans* two centuries ago by that great student of classification, Carolus Linnaeus. More recently, however, it has been renamed *Haemotobia serrata*—doubtless a more accurate but less colorful appellation.

It's Going to Sting Me!

The best case of scientific name calling, however, is the cognomen given a tiny black fly. If you've ever suffered on a spring evening through the attacks of black flies, you'll nod in high approval at the name given to one species by a disgruntled scientist. Doubtless at the end of his patience, he flatly stated the title by which it should be known from that time on: *Simulium damnosum*.

Flies, mosquitoes and their ilk are a diverse lot. They include a number of fascinating kinds: a mosquito that catches and eats other mosquitoes, for instance (now there's a *good* mosquito for you), and a spraddle-legged wingless inhabitant of my Vermont woodland who takes midwinter walks on the snow. There are horseflies so large that they are often caught in nets set for birds, and parasitic flies so small that they spend their childhood careers in the eggs of other insects. There are crane flies, stiletto flies, tropical palmetto flies, humpbacked flies, flatfooted flies—but you get the idea. All told there are about a hundred thousand known species—and authorities say less than half of them have been officially tallied.

The most infamous of the lot is the *Anopheles* mosquito, implicated in the spread of malaria. The mosquito rests (and bites) with its entire body at an angle to the surface, like a straight dart that has penetrated at a slant. Most other mosquitoes rest and feed with body parallel to the surface, head appropriately bent downward, ready for action.

If you've ever tramped the northern woods, marshes or shores in mosquito season, actually breathing the audacious little insects and getting them in your eyes like windblown dust, it's hard to believe your fortunes could sink much lower. Yet if malaria and other dread mosquito-

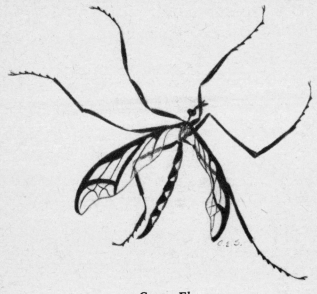

Crane Fly

borne diseases were not confined to near-tropical countries, you'd come out of the encounter with a lot more than mosquito bites. Not only that, but—believe it or not—you're under fire of only a mere fraction of the total skeeter population. Male mosquitoes, it seems, do not bite.

The female mosquito must have that sample of blood in order to develop her eggs. Her mouthparts are fitted with tiny lancets that work against each other like ratchets, forcing deep under your skin. The lancets may probe around like questing fingers, seeking a blood vessel. When she strikes home, the mosquito injects an anticlotting material so her meal will flow freely. About the time this material hits a nerve, you spring into action. Thus dinner for a mosquito may consist of a dozen or more "courses," all suddenly and precipitously terminated by the unwilling caterer, until she is filled—or flattened.

Male mosquitoes get their nourishment from the sap of plants, the nectar of flowers or the juice of fruit. You can tell male from female by the large, feathery antennae. These organs respond to her subtle odor, wafted in his direction. In some mosquitoes, at least, these complicated feelers also vibrate like a tuning fork in response to her high-pitched hum. Thus she hits him with a double-barreled allure, like a lady wearing perfume, I suppose—and carrying a school bell, just in case.

Successful, the female bestows a few dozen eggs on appropriate puddles and swamps. She's surprisingly resourceful about it. Any container with even a bit of rainwater receives the next potential population: rain barrels, discarded beverage cans, even flower vases in cemeteries. The eggs may hatch into little swimming "wigglers," which mature into more mosquitoes in as little as ten days or two weeks. So, if your vacation begins about two weeks after a drenching rain, you may have timed it perfectly—from the mosquito point of view.

Gnats and midges, cousins of the mosquitoes, have temporary aquariums, too—knotholes of trees for some midges, the cupped leaves of plants for others; pure mountain streams for some black fly gnats. And right there, I guess, is a redeeming factor; if the black flies are biting, there's good clear water nearby—even if they won't let you enjoy it.

Animals go underground, or wallow in the mud, or submerge themselves to the nostrils in a friendly pond during mosquito and gnat season. I've known a white-tailed deer to lie down in a tiny stream, forming a dam with its body. The water deepened until it flowed over the "dam," thus washing away the flies and bringing cooling relief to the deer.

You and I probably lack the patience and fortitude for such antics. Besides, we have jars and aerosols and modern roll-ons of repellent to help us. But there are a few other ways in which to lessen the visits of these animated reminders of the good old days when there was only citronella.

Mosquitoes and gnats, it seems, have certain preferences among people. Dark clothing attracts them; so does the overheated human body. Carbon dioxide gives them the clue that a living, breathing animal is near. They bite better in still air than on windy, sunny days. So, if you'd be as free of the pests as possible, wear light-colored clothes; keep calm; take a shower, perhaps, to cool you off; stay where it's light and airy. Don't breathe, either: remember the carbon dioxide!

Before departing from the mosquitoes and their relatives, one last fly should be mentioned. This is the cluster fly—that zany, bungling critter that buzzes around windows and attics on warm winter days. Sometimes you find them by the quart in an abandoned room where the sun streams in through the glass. They're really quite harmless; they are just wintering over in the hospitality of your home. During the rest of the year they live in the soil as larvae, or scatter themselves around the countryside when adult.

It's almost impossible to cluster-fly-proof your home. They find their way inside through keyholes; the chinks of bricks and cement; the spaces under clapboards. Best thing is to open the window when they want to get out, sweep

Earwig

up the remainder, and thank your lucky stars that they'll leave peacefully in the spring.

No list of disconcerting insects would be complete without mention of an uninvited import to our shores: the European earwig. Thousands of visitors to the Old World —from the GI's of World War II to today's jet-propelled tourists—have missed millions of hours of sleep because of a mythical habit of this irrepressible little insect. The earwig, so the story goes, delights in crawling into the ears of sleeping persons. It never seems to be explained how an earwig can abide the presence of the waxy secretions of the ear—which, incidentally is a natural insect repellent.

There it is, however, in the crack of the floor, apparently poised for an attack. So, if you believe what you hear, you lie awake half the night expecting an invasion—or perhaps you flounce out of the room in a huff and never grace those sleeping quarters with your presence again.

Nor is this the only virtue to which the earwig lays claim. At its nether end are two wicked-looking stilettos, like the curved jaws of a forceps. These, if you can believe what you hear, may deal a devastating sting.

As with many old wives' tales, there's a grain of truth to it all. Earwigs, secretive during the day, commonly squeeze into an opening that will just admit their dark, flattened bodies. Perhaps, on occasion, one has trotted across a pillow and poked experimentally into somebody's ear. As for the sting in the pinchers, the insect may raise its two-pronged tail threateningly if disturbed—and there's the start of *that* story.

In reality, the earwig is harmless. Its main concern is in consuming such a varied diet as flower petals, plant and animal debris, and other insects. Its "pinchers" may be used as clumsy swords during battles for some desirable female. Then, after his mate has been wooed and subdued, the male may use his erstwhile battle weapons as claspers to hold her during the final act of the undercover drama.

One more detail of the life of this intriguing insect: After she has laid her eggs, the female may stand guard or even partially curl her body over them, like a mother hen on the nest. In a few days the youngsters hatch: diminutive copies of their parents, complete with tiny tweezers and the urge to make their own mark in the world. Off they trot—perhaps even stowing away in the belongings of the tourist who packs his bags and heads home, breathing a sigh of relief that he's leaving such critters far behind.

Granted, then, that the earwig is neither bark nor bite, and the appearance of a bee or wasp does not necessarily mean the Outdoors is out, how about the other purveyors of poison—the spiders, for instance, and the scorpions and centipedes? They're lying in wait out there, too, aren't they?

They certainly are. But not for you. All in all, the members of these many-legged groups are predaceous, and feed on other creatures, thus accounting for their poison. The only time they'd use their weapons on you would be in self-defense. And if you're reasonably careful, such an occasion need probably never arise.

Consider the celebrated black widow spider, for instance. While it's true that her venom is among the most potent of animal poisons, don't let such a fact cancel out your projected visit to the country. In all of recorded medical history, there are but a few score deaths that can be laid unequivocally at the door of this pea-sized little creature, quietly living back in a corner.

Her poison is virulent, yes—but she is so shy that she'll seldom use it, except on the unfortunate creatures that fall into her web. That web, nondescript and with no apparent pattern in the weaving, is built under a lumber pile, in the hollow of a cement block, or in some dim and sheltered portion of a building. One of the favorite spots for her silken snare used to be in the corners and under the seats of the old-fashioned privy—a bit of primitive architecture that has all but disappeared as a part of the American scene.

Black widow silk, by the way, is surprisingly tough and resilient. Stronger than steel, it is scarcely affected by moisture, jarring or temperature. Single strands of the silk have long been used as cross hairs in telescopic gunsights, binoculars and microscopes. This brings up the picture of the hunter or bird-lover, squinting through his fine optical equipment—and hoping there are no black widows around.

There are even people who raise black widows for their silk. In fact, I once toyed with the idea, and carefully nurtured several dozen of them in babyfood jars. The females were shiny jet black, with all or part of an hourglass figure on their undersides in red, orange or yellow. The males were half the bulk of their well-rounded spouses—although with the same one-inch total legspan—and brown in color with yellow splotches and bands on their slender bodies and legs.

There were holes punched in the lid of each jar, and the occupant shared its quarters with a small piece of fruit. Little flies and other insects, attracted by the fruit, entered through the holes and blundered into the spiderweb.

Despite the brilliance of such an ingenious self-feeding operation, I had almost no success in getting my foundation stock to reproduce. When presented to each other the prospective mates showed either (1) indifference, or (2) an undue amount of interest—resulting in the eating of one spider by the other. Usually the large female would be the winner (hence the name "black widow"), although one liberated male managed to do away with two potential brides before I retired him in alarm.

Just about this time I learned that the optical companies already had their own suppliers, anyway, so my scheme to corner the cross hair market fizzled out. However, it wasn't a complete failure: specimens of the black widow, suitably labeled and inebriated forever in alcohol, now reside in the collections of the University of Vermont, Middlebury College, and in what some people must consider a startling display on my own shelves.

Retiring as it is, the black widow gets around. It has been reported from nearly all parts of the continental United States and southern Canada. And no use staying home to avoid a confrontation with *Latrodectus mactans*, either; it can be found in cellars, elevator shafts and recessed basement windows. One time, when Peg and I were visiting Dick and Freda King in North Carolina, we found a black widow in one out of every three sunken gas meter boxes, right there on the lawns of Raleigh.

On the outside chance that you should reach an incautious hand into the spider's parlor—or if you pay a vist to one of the rare outdoor privies that's already occupied by a black widow, and get bitten in the bargain—the bite will feel like little more than a pinprick. The toxin affects the nerves rapidly, however, so there's little help in the usual "snakebite" cures. Get medical aid at once, as sweating, cramps and a sore and rigid abdomen can quickly follow. The abdomen may be so painful that more than one person has been operated on for acute appendicitis following a half-noticed black widow bite.

If bitten, by the way, be sure of your spider. Capture it if possible—even if it's the worse for wear because you swatted it. You may save yourself unnecessary worry, as scores of harmless spiders are black in color, and will defend themselves if molested. A nip from a harmless spider may hurt for a few moments, but is scarcely more troublesome than a mosquito bite.

The brown recluse spider (*Loxosceles reclusa*) of the south and west may cause a wound that is stubborn to heal, but many people have been bitten with no harm at all. Sometimes called the fiddleback, this spider is light brown with a pattern resembling that of a tiny violin in darker brown on the head. About the same size as the black widow (with a half-inch-long body), it lives behind furniture and in the corners of rooms, where it has long been the target of the fastidious housewife and her broom. Now, following the notoriety gained since a number of severe bites in the 1950's, every brown spider immediately becomes a fiddleback. This, it would seem, puts us in imminent danger of invasion.

Well, 'tain't so. The United States Department of Agriculture vows that the brown recluse has been around for years. With modern communication, we hear about its bite sooner and oftener. Indeed—if we can twist a familiar phrase around—to the jittery home owner, believing is seeing.

As for tarantulas, scorpions and centipedes, these creatures reach their greatest numbers in warmer climates than this book attempts to cover. There are, however, junior editions of each—the hairy wolf spiders, or "northern tarantulas"; matchhead-sized "false scorpions"; two-inch centipedes—in the cooler sections of our continent.

The tarantulas, among the most dreaded of spiders because of their hairy appearance and large size, have labored for centuries under bad publicity. Most of them, for all their fearsome looks, are harmless to man. Their bite may be painful, but scarcely serious. A friend of mine, Mrs. Patty Hier, once brought me a South American tarantula that had been found in a shipment of bananas. Called the bird spider because its large size allows it to capture and eat small birds and mice, the creature was a female as big as a Ping-Pong ball, with legs able to overstretch a saucer.

At first the spider was a veritable spitfire, fighting at

anything thrust into her terrarium. She soon became tame, however, and never again attempted to bite in the years that I had her. I took her with me on lecture tours, and several dozen of the braver members of my audiences handled her without a mishap.

Her food consisted of a portion of meat or a roadside-killed mouse about once a month. She'd mince it up between powerful fangs, injecting a digestive fluid through its hollow points and sucking up the resultant soup. The mouse would gradually get smaller as she worked it over, until it was reduced to a pile of bones and hair the size of a grape in twenty-four hours.

One morning I found her dead in her terrarium, apparently from nothing more complicated than old age. I placed her remains in a large display case. She is still there today—a denizen of my private collection. Even now, some ten years after her demise, people still pay her visits, filing past her glass-covered casket as if she were some matriarch lying in state.

The local counterparts of Arachne, as we called her, after the girl who was changed to a spider in the Greek legend, are known as wolf spiders. They chase their prey (hence the name) and rely on strength and agility rather than lethal poison to win them a dinner. The "tarantulas" of our western states are often large wolf spiders. The sudden materialization of one of these outside your tent or trailer or in your yard might be a greater shock than any poison it could administer. After all, it seems, such a frightful-looking creature *must* be deadly. In truth, however, the bite of even these large spiders is scarcely as bad as a bee sting.

In some parts of the world the spider is considered a

sign of good luck. Householders in warm climates welcome a good wolf spider for its effect on the cockroach population. Asiatic people feel fortunate if they meet a spider; it's about like finding a lucky penny. In certain tribes, one consults the spider and the shape of its web for a prediction of the weather.

Such a lucky omen reaches the height of perfection in the Near East. A newly married couple will be abundantly blessed by the presence of a spider. And the sooner the blessing starts, apparently, the better it is—so the salubrious creature is placed right in the bed of the newlyweds.

Lacking such sentiments, however, and before you pack up and leave the country to the arachnids (the spiders and their relatives), remember that they're just as much a part of the outdoors as that tree, that rock, the sky. In fact they were here first—by some half-billion years, the archeologists tell us. It is we who are the intruders.

Those other arachnids, the scorpions, look like some sort of a landlubber lobster. There are about two dozen species in the United States, almost entirely confined to hot, dry regions. Generally shy and secretive, they hide under bark and stones during the heat of day, coming out at dusk to feed on insects and other small creatures. On occasion, the folds and confines of a sleeping bag or tarpaulin make a good place to hide, so it's well to check such items before crawling in for the night. A scorpion in the shoe is an exhilarating event: one reason the range-riding cowboy often slept with his boots on.

Scorpion stings are painful, true, and any persistent reaction—rapid breathing, nausea, excessive salivation—should receive prompt medical care, as people have died from the effect. A majority of such victims are children or elderly persons. Most stings, however, are not serious. The sting is usually administered as the creature arches its tail forward, over its back, stabbing with the pointed tip.

There is one bad offender, however. This is the Durango scorpion (*Centruroides*), only a couple of inches long. It's especially common in the Mexican state of Durango, and has been responsible for hundreds of deaths, mainly children. Besides the acute pain of its sting, there's a general fuzziness of the senses, and a rise in temperature. So serious is the sting that in some places south of the border a bounty for two cents for male scorpions and two-and-a-half cents for females has been paid.

In my own state of Vermont, the best we can muster up is a squat creature known as a pseudo-scorpion. Scarcely a quarter-inch long, it resembles a scorpion minus the tail

Pseudo-Scorpion

but retaining the pinchers. Although it is completely harmless to man, it looks bizarre enough to trigger half a dozen telephone calls a year from people who ask me about "this thing that looks like a cross between a scorpion and a tick, crawling right up my wall."

The ticks, by the way, are leathery, flattened arachnids with an astonishing stomach capacity. Most adult ticks are less than a quarter-inch long—that is, when they're empty. After they have attached themselves to a host and filled up with blood, they may attain the size of a marble.

Ticks rarely cause pain or sensation when attaching to your unsuspecting person, and may produce little discomfort at all. Yet so traumatic can be the discovery of a tick embedded in your skin, that many people will stay out of woods and bushes during "tick season" (spring and early summer) rather than come in contact with them. And right there, perhaps, if we could somehow get outside our own ego and look at ticks from a non-human standpoint, is a big "plus" for them: they keep people from forever having their own way, all the time

Ticks have no wings, and possess only slow powers of locomotion. They cannot hop onto a convenient host animal as can a flea, nor can they fly about in search of a handout, as does the mosquito. The way of life of a tick is a risky one, indeed.

Slowly, laboriously, the tick climbs from the ground up the stem and branch of a selected weed or bush. It creeps to the tip of a leaf and takes up a position, forelegs outstretched. There it remains, for hours, days, weeks, waiting for the chance-in-a-million to snag onto the fur of a passing animal—or the clothing that adorns your unsuspecting person. If it chooses the wrong bush it may starve to death.

If fortune smiles and the creature's hitchhiking efforts are successful, it still has a ways to go. A scrape against the next bush may dislodge it again—and the whole long wait must begin once more. Or, as it creeps about in search of a spot to bite, it may be ousted by its intended host.

As it crawls along, seeking a suitable place for a nip, a perambulating tick can scarcely be felt beneath your clothing. When it settles down, it may take minutes—even hours—to become firmly attached. Many ticks produce a mild anesthetic so that even the slight irritation of the bite cannot be noticed. If undetected, the tick feeds for a few days and then drops off. A disease known as spotted fever may be carried by ticks, but cases of it are rare.

The best way to check for ticks if you've been exposed to them is to examine yourself in the Altogether before a full-length mirror. Pay especial attention to your scalp and hairline; the mild toxin produced by some ticks may bring on a local numbness when it's released that close to the brain. Full-fledged cases of such numbness may involve the nervous system and are known as tick paralysis and, on a few occasions, have been serious enough to cause death.

Some species of ticks, it is true, can carry disease. Texas fever has killed thousands of cattle. Rocky Mountain spotted fever affects man and animals. But the worst effect on most of us is a malady known as acariphobia—just plain fear of the critters. When you suffer from it, every little touch of your clothing seems to be a tick headed for lunch. You spend anxious moments looking for a tick that isn't there. Forests and fields become peopled with them—all waiting, arms outstretched, to embrace you as you pass by.

Once the head of a tick is ensconced in your skin, the

creature is a bit tricky to remove. Discourage it by touching the end of its body with lighter fluid, or by bringing a lighted cigarette close to it—but not both at the same instant. The uncomfortable tick will release its hold and will back out by itself or can be slowly dislodged. Sometimes you can carefully scrape it off intact with a knife. Otherwise, if you merely pull it away by the body, the head may remain buried and create a local infection.

Ticks, by the way, are actually large members of the mite family. Some kinds of these latter tiny creatures, such as the chiggers, have the engaging habit of partially burrowing into the skin, leaving you with little itchy red souvenirs of a sojourn in a grassy meadow. "Sleep may be difficult," announces one book about such critters—which, to anyone who has ever played host to these little "red bugs," is a marvelous understatement.

Sulphur ointment helps cut the mites' visit short. A baking-soda paste aids in quelling the itch. There are also pain-deadening creams that can be smeared on for a few days until the mite, in its own good time, moves on.

Incidentally, severe attacks of certain mites on animals may cause a condition known as mange. Should you spot a mangy fox or rabbit in the outdoors, there's little need to worry that you're next in line. The mange mites are generally much fussier than that and don't usually care for people.

Most of these little invaders are just within the limit of visibility. The common bright red mites of lawns and meadows are much larger, ranging up to the size of a grain of rice. They capture tiny creatures of their grassy world and hence are harmless—unless you're smaller than they are.

One parting shot: The caboose, as it were, of this train of insects, spiders and their allies—collectively known as arthropods, or jointed-legged creatures. Last in line come the leggiest of all: the centipedes and millipedes.

We'll dismiss the latter first. These cylindrical, hard-shelled creatures are commonly known as thousand-legged worms. Touch a millipede and it curls up into a flat spiral until danger is past. Or, in some species, it may whip back and forth, scattering an almond-smelling scent upon the air. To us the scent is merely peculiar, but to an over-zealous spider or beetle it may be a jolting surprise. The scent is hydrogen cyanide, a poison gas that doubtless persuades many a predator to seek easier prey.

The millipede itself is harmless; it merely feeds on plant material, which makes it quite inoffensive—as long as the plants are growing in the other fellow's garden.

And, lastly, the centipedes. These flattened creatures, going the gamut in colors from white through reds and browns to black, consist of a string of segments, each bearing a pair of legs. Sometimes they are impressive, indeed —almost a foot long in some tropical species, and with the hundred or more legs that give them their name. In spite of all those appendages, however, they apparently never get confused. Some can run as fast as a person's leisurely walk.

Centipedes are predaceous, with the first legs modified into poison claws. They can pinch with those claws, and give a painful bite, but they're just like most of the rest of this cast of characters; they bite in self-defense. The poison goes away quickly—at least for you and me. Insects and snails and slugs may not be so lucky. Like countless generations before them, they've been serving up unwilling meals to centipedes, scientists tell us, since the days of the dinosaurs.

And there you have one look at the arthropod: the stinging, biting, short-tempered ones. We'll meet a few more of them later on. In fact, they're in the very next chapter—just lying there, waiting in ambush.

3 ·...And Creepers and Crawlers

Well, you made it so far; you went out among all those spiders and insects and lived to tell the tale. Before we leave such creatures completely, however, some parting words about a few more of their relatives. After all, just because something does not sting or bite is no guarantee you'll feel easy when it's around. Sometimes its mere presence gives you the jitters.

Hence, this chapter. It's about more insects, I must confess, but it will be a short one—not because there's little further to say but because there is so much. Right now, biologists state there are about a million species of insects known to science. Estimates of the eventual total—when they're all counted—vary from twice that figure to eight times as much.

That's a lot of creeping and buzzing and humming. And since, despite his success with such creatures as the dodo and the passenger pigeon, man has not yet been able to exterminate a single insect species, chances are the critters will be with us a long, long time.

Obviously we cannot even list them all. Just to name them at the rate of one per second, night and day without sleeping would take one to three months—depending on whose estimate you believe. With such a staggering number, all we can do is pry into a few of the more familiar lives. Some of these we met in the last chapter, but there are others to reckon with, as well. They scuttle out from under your lawn chair, cuddle right into your blanket party, contemplate your siesta from the top of the hedge.

Among such irrepressible visitors is that holdover from prehistoric times, the cockroach. Roaches have been found on every continent. They make their way into all phases of our existence. They've been shooed out of the best hotels and hastily evicted from luxury liners. Cockroaches were blasted aloft in early biosatellites to determine how animal life would withstand space travel. They stood it in great shape, taking the stress of blast-off and the strain of confinement with equal aplomb. And one of the most impressive insect fossils ever found was the imprint of a creature nearly a foot long. Dating back to the coal age it was—you guessed it—a giant cockroach.

As a student of animal physiology I dutifully peered into the durable insect's innards to discover what made it tick. One of my classmates spent an entire semester teaching a rabble of roaches to distinguish right from left in a simple maze. She succeeded, too. They passed the test with flying colors, thus proving what any householder who has tried to outfox them with trick baits and fancy traps already knows: cockroaches can learn.

But you've got to hand it to them. They have survived everything, and they keep coming back for more. Clean up your kitchen and they'll sneak down to the cellar.

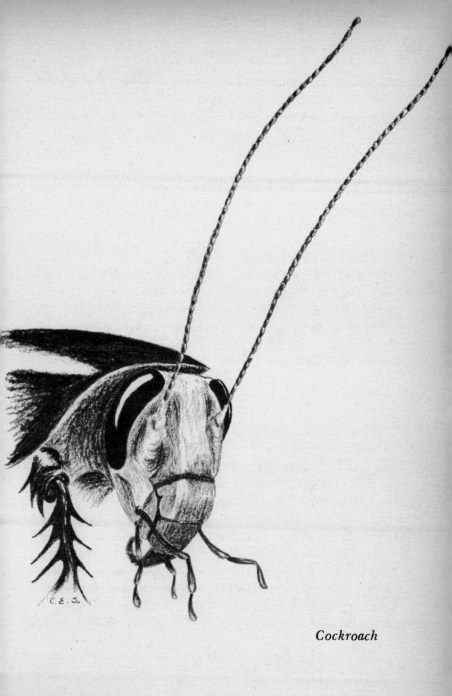

Cockroach

Brush out the basement and they go to the garage. Wherever we establish a home, chances are that the blatant creatures could be in on the housewarming.

Since roaches don't spring up through spontaneous generation, but obviously have to have come from somewhere, the last known port of call gets the credit. Thus we have the interesting whodunit with regard to a common small house roach. In New York City this creature is often called the Croton bug because it materialized during the construction of New York City's Croton water system. Scientists had already officially named it, however: *Blattella germanica*, the German cockroach. Go to Germany and they pass the buck, too. There it's known as the Russian roach. And the Russians lay the guilt on everybody.

Small matter, actually, where any roach came from before you inherited it. As some wag has pointed out, it's no sin to have roaches—it's just a sin to keep them.

Since the living is best for roaches where there is dampness, darkness, food and warmth, much can be done to make things less hospitable. Take out the garbage often, fix that leaky water pipe, sweep up under the sink: it sounds like someone's list of Saturday chores, but it'll do much to keep a home roach-free.

Poisonous baits and sprays help, too. Spread a powder such as rotenone where the insects will walk through it; the powder is harmless to pets and children. When the roach licks itself (it's as fussy in personal cleanliness as a cat), it swallows grains of the powder. Soon its ability to breathe and carry on normal bodily processes is lessened, and it turns up its toes—all six of them. Boric acid powder, also relatively harmless, likewise is death on roaches. Sodium fluoride powder is even more effective, but is poisonous and must be used with care. As the roach scurries to its hiding place, it trails some of the powder with it, spreading woe among the rest of its family back home.

And "family" is almost the right word here, too. Although there are few insects beyond the bees, wasps and termites that actively care for their young, the cockroach shows just a smattering of family life. When the female produces eggs, she carries them around in a case attached to the end of her body; thus she is her own babysitter. The active little youngsters, dashing about like a troop of Brownie Scouts, occasionally return to the nest locality for a "kiss"—actually, a chance to share a drop of food still remaining on the mouthparts of some adult. And now and again one roach will groom another—a fanciful resemblance, I suppose, to a mother straightening the hair of her youngsters and putting their clothes in order. Such togetherness is an oddity in the insect world, most of whose inhabitants either ignore or fight with each other.

In themselves, these little individualists are quite harmless to human beings. The dozen or so cockroach species that occasionally share our dwellings do not bite. They seldom carry any maladies that would affect us. Most of what they eat is material we're through with, anyway. And that last item, perhaps, is the point: if we're wasteful or lazy, or slow to dispose of our debris, it's not long before they tell us about it. Luckily the creatures are secretive in their habits and seldom venture out except under cover of darkness, or chances are they'd tell the world, too.

Cockroaches have numerous relatives; among them the grasshoppers, crickets and walking sticks. Few of us, it seems, are perturbed by the presence of grasshoppers and crickets. Among the most musical of all insects, these creatures make the fields and roadsides shimmer with their songs in summer and autumn.

The walking sticks seldom produce much of a reaction, either, except in certain parts of the south, where they're known as "devil's horses" and "mule killers." A few of them have the alarming habit of squirting an irritating but harmless fluid from glands behind the neck region; this doubtless gives them their local reputation. In more northern climes, they seem to be content with no real means of defense except to resemble twigs so closely that "they look like what they ain't, Mr. Rood," as one of my general science students assured me.

The praying mantis is another story. A bit like the walking stick in appearance but a world apart in behavior, it is a creature of steel-trap forelegs, heart-shaped face and goggly eyes. One of the largest of insects, with antics to match its bizarre appearance, the mantis can hold its own in almost any company. I've seen it confront a robin with such a threatening display that the bird fled in confusion. A friend of mine has a movie of a battle between a mantis and a frog, with the contest ending in a draw. And the first of these insects I ever saw was a defiant creature that stood its ground right in the middle of State Street in Hartford, Connecticut—stopping pedestrians and tying up traffic for ten minutes.

A mantis may give you pause, too, when you come across it on your rosebush. Wings half spread, spiny forelegs raised in warning, owlish face scrutinizing you, it makes you feel as if you're being sized up as the next victim. If you step to one side or the other, you get a further surprise: the mantis can turn its head. It follows your every move as if you were a TV commercial.

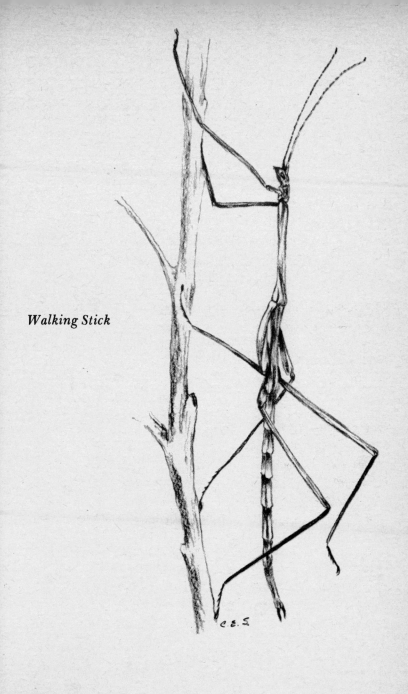

Walking Stick

Few people attempt to call its bluff. And in truth, its actions are often more than a pretense. If escape is open, the mantis may hop to another branch, but if you have it cornered, it will stand and fight. Indeed, it may even carry the battle to you, opening those forelegs like a jackknife and taking a flying leap at your outstretched finger. It cannot hurt you, however; its grip is intended merely to hold rather than to harm. After fencing with you a bit, it seems to decide that discretion is, indeed, the better part of valor. Abandoning the struggle, it tries to flee. So there's really no menace to a mantis—unless you're a cricket or a butterfly.

Speaking of butterflies, some of these dainty creatures and their moth cousins can give you quite a start—at least when they're caterpillars. In fact, there are caterpillars that can make you wish you'd never met them. As a boy I knew the little trick of dropping a woolly-bear caterpillar down the neck of a classmate. The scratchy hairs can make an itchy rash, while the sensation of that fuzzy lump curled up south of the shoulder blades is guaranteed to liven up any classroom. Not that *I* ever did anything like this, of course—I just remember that it happened.

The woolly-bear caterpillar is the young of a small nondescript yellowish moth (*Isia isabella*). It is also the famous winter-weather prophet. Black at both ends and brown in the middle, the fuzzy creatures hurry along in autumn as if in desperate search of a good winter hiding place. Soothsayers gifted with the art of caterpillar-reading scrutinize the woolly bears, fore and aft and middle. If the two black ends are abbreviated, with a large expanse of center section, there'll be a long winter that begins and ends abruptly. Some experts disagree; the big brown belt means a brown, open (snowless) winter. A narrower midriff means a shorter season.

A good caterpillar watcher will view several dozen of the creatures before he ventures his prognostication. In the little Vermont town where I live there are three such clairvoyants. Their findings are sometimes a bit at variance —a fault, no doubt, of the observers rather than the flawless insects themselves.

The woolly bear, with its black-brown-black coloration, is but one of a large number of fuzzy caterpillars. Some are all one color, some are marked with splotches and patches. The saddleback caterpillar has a green patch on its body (the saddle cloth) in the center of which is a brown spot (the saddle). It's covered with bristly hairs that will leave a welt even if they merely brush against you. Such a delightful experience is immortalized in the last part of its scientific name: *Sibine stimulea*—the stimulator.

Best suggestion in dealing with unknown insects, I guess, is to go slow around any fuzzy caterpillar. Touch it only with the tough skin of your palm or fingers. Those hairs serve primarily to discourage birds, yes—but they can do an equally good job on you.

Repellent hairdos are just openers in the bag of tricks possessed by the caterpillar world. The hairs may be reduced to large bristles or spines. Touch the warty, spiny green larva of the huge cecropia moth (*Samia cecropia*) if you dare; it is harmless, but it must take a hungry bird to ignore all those bumps and carbuncles.

The velvet-brown Regal moth (*Citheronia regalis*) has a green caterpillar about the size of a sausage. Called the hickory horned devil, it would doubtless be delicious

Hickory Horned Devil

except for two or more pairs of wicked-looking horns behind its head. When disturbed, the devil tenses and tucks its head down, thrusting those half-inch horns out as if to impale you on the spot. Aggravate it further and it lashes around so that you retire in haste to avoid getting skewered like a shish kebab.

Swallowtail butterfly (*Papilio* species) larvae have fleshy, evil-smelling "horns" that they suddenly inflate from a pocket behind the head when they're threatened. Other caterpillars are adorned with huge, staring "eyes"—actually only spots of color—that make them look like some sort of abbreviated snake that's all head and no body. Harmless, these creatures, but so convincing that you let them travel unmolested—which, of course, is the general idea.

You'll find false eyes on the backs of beetles, too. The eyed elater is nearly the length of the last two joints of your little finger, and displays a huge pair of velvety-black "eyes" on its grayish body. The eyes, of course, are sightless, although a tropical species has a couple of luminescent "pupils" in their centers, so they glow in the dark.

If the eyes don't fool you, the beetle draws in its legs and antennae and just lies there, thus possibly escaping notice. If you still do not leave, *it* will leave—by leaps and bounds. The term "elater" means "jumper," and by snapping one portion of its body against another—somewhat as you snap your fingers—the insect propels itself as much as a foot into the air. At the same time there's a loud "click"—hence, the popular name of click beetle. And away it goes, like a piece of popcorn gone berserk.

Its leaps are without direction, however, so it doesn't get very far. But such behavior may take it out of harm's way. Even if it is captured and eaten, the heavily armored beetle most likely keeps on clicking for a while—a memorable lesson, doubtless, for its captor.

There's another click beetle resembling this one, but the eyespots are fuzzy and indistinct. Looking at the scientific names of the two we find that even entomologists have their fun. The beetle with the fine, clear eyespots is appropriately known as *Alaus oculatus*—"the one with eyes." Its faulty visioned relative is *Alaus myops*—and a myopic creature, of course, is one that doesn't see too well.

You have probably contemplated other click beetles as they performed on a spadeful of freshly turned earth. You may have seen their larvae, too: glossy, enameled-yellow creatures of the soil known as wireworms. Touch a wireworm and it flips around as if to give you a nasty bite. Like its parents, however, it's only bluff. Most wireworms are vegetarians.

"Bluff," indeed, is the byword for a number of beetles. Longhorned beetles whip their astonishing antennae— sometimes four inches long—in your direction. Rove beetles elevate the rear portion of their abdomen as if threatening to sting. Locust-borer beetles carry the illusion further, as they are colored an arresting hornet yellow-and-black. Some ground beetles even buzz like a hornet; one time I watched our two dogs solemnly following a ground beetle as it scurried for shelter along a driveway. Every time they came near, it buzzed its agitation and made them jump back in bewilderment.

Then there are the "bluffers" that aren't: they can back up their threats with action. Stag beetles can give you a respectable pinch with those mandibles, sometimes branched like the antlers of a stag. Rhinocerous beetles can pinch, too, or give you a boost with their horns, located behind the head. Tiger beetles, those swiftly-running creatures of brilliant metallic colors, will rear up on their hind legs at you if they're cornered. In case you don't get the message, they may even attack with outspread jaws. Once I saw a bright green tiger beetle vanquish a lady's poodle on a Long Island beach.

One of the most effective performances is that of the bombardier beetle. This insect bears a couple of sacs of

Stag Beetle

fluid at its nether end. Disturb it and it raises its rear artillery in your direction. There's a distinct little "pop" —and a tiny cloud of ill-smelling gas explodes just to its rear. The little blue beetle with the rust-colored head can fire half a dozen times: not bad, considering it's only half an inch long.

These are just a few of the beetles that may startle you when you first meet them. A bit similar in appearance, but related only because they are insects, too, are the true bugs. Technically, the term "bug" may be applied only to those insects with a piercing, sucking beak. Thus we have squash bugs and stinkbugs—but a ladybug is really a beetle while a pillbug is a small cousin to the crabs and lobsters.

Now, the bedbug—that's a true bug. Thin as paper when empty, and capable of hiding in the merest crack, the bedbug has been called man's closest companion. It has a small, pointed beak with which it takes a quick sample of your blood in three or four minutes.

Sometime in your career—if it hasn't happened more than once already—you'll be in a second-rate hotel or other snuggery of doubtful grace. There you may spend half the night turning the light on and off and flinging the covers wildly because of the real or imagined presence of *Cimex lectularius*. Such precipitous behavior may upset the schedules of a few of these creatures, but the dire effects of their bite are more imagined than real. Despite its fearsome reputation, the bedbug affects most people little more than a mosquito. Many people do not feel it at all. No single disease has ever been laid at its door, either —except, of course, an outsize case of insomnia.

So, should you find yourself in such a situation, relax, if you can. Many people lose more blood when they're shaving. Besides, the management will charge you for the room tomorrow, anyway.

To keep the bugs at bay, cleanliness is a prime virtue. Then, too, a dust known as pyrethrum will often do the job. Pyrethrum, incidentally, is a good answer to many an insect problem; it's practically harmless to other creatures. It's an organic substance, derived from a relative of those pungent chrysanthemums in your garden. Thus, in these days of return to basics, it's a natural.

As a temporary measure, set each leg of the bed in a jar cover containing water. As bedbugs have no wings, the water will prevent a floor-borne invasion from nearby furniture during the night. But don't forget to remove the jar lids in the morning, if you're a guest in these questionable quarters. Or maybe you'd better leave them in place as a subtle hint.

There are other true bugs that occasionally zero in for an attack. Sometimes their attentions seem only to be a whim: the conenose bug, for instance, that pursues household insects but may sample your sleeping person in passing. Or the stinkbug, that shield-shaped insect with the repugnant but harmless smell, that abandons its caterpillar diet long enough to prod you with that soda-straw mouthpiece. Not fussy in the least, the stinkbug may also puncture the tissues of the nearest plant, thus feeding impartially on the two most important fluids in the living world: the sap of plants and the blood of animals.

Enough, perhaps, about bugs and no-bugs—for a while, at least. They'll keep cropping up in this book, however, just as in real life. I remember one unknown critter, for instance, that shared an apartment with Peg and me shortly after we were married. It lived behind the knotty pine paneling of the wall, and joined us nightly by poking two long antennae in our direction through a tiny knothole. The hole was obviously too small to admit whatever body was behind it, and so there they were, hour after hour, night after night—two companionable feelers, gently waving a greeting.

Those antennae bid us farewell in the morning and welcomed us home at night. We never knew who owned them, but they were a good reminder that if there's one thing you can tell about insects, it is this:

You can never tell about them.

4 · ...And Scuttlers and Slinkers

People who know about such things tell us we start life with only two basic fears: the fear of loud noises and the fear of falling. All other dreads and dismays have to be learned. The apprehension that follows when you've driven through a stoplight, the shivers that come when the boss calls you in for a conference, and the mental paralysis that strikes when the teacher springs a quiz—all of these instant reactions can be laid, like a foundling, right at the doorstep of civilization.

Part of these feelings stem from personal experience; events in the past that have made a lasting impression. A friend of mine is afraid of bridges; not of heights, but of bridges themselves. As a girl, she saw a suspension bridge collapse with a shriek of tortured steel during a flood. Today the sound and sight of that bridge are still with her, and she becomes ill if she crosses anything bigger than a culvert.

"I know it's foolish, Ron," she admitted, "but I cannot help it. Even though I live only a couple of hours from

Long Island, I've been there only once—and that was by boat. I'd rather die than go over any of those big bridges."

Other people have other fears: common ones like riding in elevators and flying on airplanes; and not-so-common, like a terror I once had of the little bird known as the cedar waxwing. As a toddler I accidentally blundered into a bush that held its nest; the bird's indignation, coupled with a withering attack, left me shaken for years to come.

So it is with most of the creatures in this book—at least the ones that bother *you*. Your parent shuddered at worms, say—and you got the shudders, too. Somebody dropped a garden slug down your neck at school, and you've been terrified of slugs ever since. Great Aunt Julie practically foams at the mouth when she sees a snake—and you take leave of your senses, too. Such fear, although acquired and learned from someone else, is nonetheless real. It sort of recalls the gentleman who showed hesitation in making up his mind, whereby he was jokingly asked if he was a man or a mouse.

"I guess I'm a man," he replied. "My wife is afraid of mice."

Well, let's take mice, while we're at it. For good measure, we'll also include their cousins the rats. And that's quite a measure, too: more than a thousand species of mice and rats, if you count them all. One out of every five living mammals, it seems, is a rat or a mouse.

Listing every mouselike (or ratlike) creature, you'd include the gentle, appealing little deer mouse along with its webfooted cousin, the muskrat. Your global roster would embrace such creatures as the jerboas—which look like some kind of improbable alliance between a rabbit and a kangaroo—plus a scampering of spiny mice, dormice and fishing rats. Add several dozen gerbils, hamsters, pack rats and a few hundred fellow nibblers and you have an assortment big enough to satisfy the most avid myophobe —which term means *you*, in case you're afraid of mice.

I was a myophobe myself once, briefly. Several years ago I was riding with my son, Tom, along a country road. As we rounded a bend, we spotted a brown object the size of a grapefruit. Drawing closer, we realized it was a half-grown muskrat, huddled at the edge of the road.

The nearest water was half a mile away. Somehow the little fellow had made a wrong turn, and now he looked lost. I figured he could use some help in getting back to his own element. Stopping the car, I instructed Tom to go around behind him to cut off his escape. I advanced on him with a cardboard box which, at the proper moment, I'd clap down over him.

Everything went according to plan. Tom cut off the muskrat's escape, all right. I descended on him perfectly, too. Then, while Tom waved his hands to distract the creature, I plunked the box square on top of the muskrat.

That, however, is as far as the strategy had been plotted. And, as it turned out, there was one little flaw: the box was split along one corner.

As I bore down triumphantly on the imprisoned muskrat, the split gaped open. The box collapsed, and out poured the indignant rodent, madder than a boiled owl. Tom, faithfully following the only instructions he'd been given, waved his arms and shouted, thereby herding the muskrat in my direction. Teeth chattering, the raging rat headed for me.

I stumbled backward, holding the flattened box like a lion tamer's chair. Tom, bless his heart, followed right behind the muskrat, surrounding him at every point but straight ahead—right toward me The muskrat squeaked its defiance, drew its legs up beneath it—and leaped.

That did it. Making one ineffectual swipe with the floppy cardboard at the darting rodent, I turned and fled. Back toward the car I raced, pursued by two pounds of gristle and muscle and razor-sharp teeth.

Or so I thought. I could almost feel those incisors chomping down on my unprotected calf, somewhere between the bottom of my Bermudas and the top of my socks. But when, after a clever feint toward the left followed by a brilliant maneuver to the right, I turned to face my pursuer, he was nowhere in sight. Once escape was offered, he'd scurried away into the grass.

It must have been quite a performance; scarcely worthy of "that man who writes all the nature books," as a small fan once introduced me to another, but it was the best I could muster at the time. Mercifully, and to my everlasting gratitude, Tom did not even crack a smile.

"They sure are fast, Dad," he remarked laconically, as we got back in the car. "Never knew muskrats could be so quick." He probably never knew his father could be so quick, either.

So, when you admit that a mouse or a rat has given you an uneasy moment, you have my sympathy. I have been there myself.

One of the problems with these rodents, I believe, is the very one that almost laid me low: they scuttle. If they'd amble, or trot, or even run like a cat, say, an unrehearsed meeting with them would be less perilous to your wits. But they seem to have only two speeds: Fast and Stop. Such behavior doubtless protects them from their many

enemies; a sudden dash and an abrupt halt may cause
many a hawk or owl to overshoot the mark. However, such
antics sure can play havoc with your equanimity if you're
not prepared.

Another problem with mice and rats—and for that matter, rodents in general—is they are gnawing, gnawing,
forever gnawing. Indeed, the name "rodent" means "one
who eats away," and it's no accident that the words "cor-
rode" and "erosion" have the same Latin base. So when
you picture one of these creatures you're apt to conjure
up a specter with long, horrendous, ever-busy choppers.

There's a good reason for the incessant chewing of the
Rodentia, however; those front teeth are constantly growing. Gnawing is necessary to keep them worn down. If one
tooth is broken so it does not grind against its mate in the
other jaw, the undamaged tooth lengthens out of proportion. It becomes first an annoyance, and then a threat
because the unfortunate rodent cannot eat properly.
Finally it will starve—if the oversized tusk, growing in a
circle, has not already penetrated its brain.

As to potential peril from rats and mice to your unprotected person, there is, admittedly, a possibility that you
may receive a nip if you become too familiar with them.
Some, like the common house rat, can be downright
unfriendly at times. A lady I know cornered a rat in a
garage, poked at it with a broom—and fled as the rodent
climbed the handle.

I remember, too, our placid old cow, dreamily grazing
in the meadow until she happened to crop a tuft of grass
that sheltered a nest of meadow mice. Uprooted, the lesser
members of the mouse family darted off into the neighbor-
ing grass while their dispossessed mother fought a rear-

guard action. Squeaking her defiance, she raised up on tiny hind legs at the startled bovine. Daisy, backing away in haste, put several yards between herself and the peppery rodent. Then, apparently weighing the probability of a nip in the nose if she trespassed again, she turned aside and mowed a swath in a respectful curve around the forbidden nest.

The chunky-bodied, gray-brown, short-tailed meadow mouse can be like that. Not ordinarily, of course, but when it finds itself in danger. On the other hand its grassroots neighbor, the whitefooted mouse, may adopt a different approach. Slender of body, long of tail, with its warm brown upper fur, white belly and pink feet, this graceful member of the deermouse tribe will seldom stand and fight. Disturb its nest and you may get a surprise of a different nature.

Suppose you have just lifted an old log, say, and discovered the soft ball of down and grasses, which is the nest of this peaceful woodland resident. Or perhaps you attempted to clean out the birdhouse in readiness for this year's guests, and have discovered that a whitefoot has usurped the box. The first evidence you may have that the nest is inhabited might be an inquisitive pair of liquid dark eyes, surmounted by large, shell-thin ears. A dozen long, sensitive whiskers may twitch your way for a moment, followed by disappearance of the mouse. The whole nest may shake in agitation; then out bursts the mouse in a dash for safety.

She may not be alone, however. Much of her time in the nest is spent nursing the youngsters. So tightly do their sucking mouths cling to her nipples that, in her flight to freedom, she drags her babies along with her. An emergency hole is in readiness nearby, and you gape at the improbable sight as the little family cluster wobbles and struggles and bumps along the ground to safety.

Often one or two of her half dozen youngsters will shake loose as she runs. Or they may have been too large for such a performance in the first place. She still dashes to safety, but in a few moments her courage returns and she is back to look for strays. If you pick up one of the pink, blind, helpless youngsters it may squeak in surprise. Cup it in your hand and the mother will run up to the crying captive. Taking her stand just inches from the little prisoner, she sits on her haunches, front paws held as if in supplication, while she awaits the return of her youngster. Open your fist and she picks the baby up with her teeth and scampers away.

Once you have seen such a demonstration, and once the reason for all that scuttling and gnawing is made apparent, you may look at rodents in a new light. Despite their tremendous numbers (there may be more than a hundred mice per acre of a well-populated meadow), each is an individual. To learn about their ways is to give a new dimension to the outdoors.

I'll long remember pitching the tent in a Midwestern meadow, for instance. Our family had noticed a pair of ground squirrels nearby as we set up camp, but had paid little attention to them. After supper we washed the dishes, spread our sleeping bags out on the canvas floor of the tent, and prepared for a needed sleep after a long day of traveling.

Sleep did not come quite as fast as we'd anticipated. One after another, we felt odd little nudges and pushes up through the canvas beneath our sleeping bags. Apparently

Ground Squirrel

we had carefully spread ourselves right over the home of the ground squirrels, and they were exploring their tunnels, raising the ceiling where our weight had compressed the earth. After half an hour they had repaired the damage—and then we all settled down for good.

Had we not noticed those ground squirrels before dark, we might have scared ourselves out of a night's sleep.

After all, our imaginations might have asked, what could cause such a disturbance? Moles? Gophers? Some form of huge beetle? No problem if it was one of these. But— heaven forbid—what if it had been a rattlesnake?

This, I guess, is the point when you're out among all those scuttlers and slinkers: they were there first; it is *we* who are the intruders. Almost without exception, they have no nefarious designs on our tender persons. They desire little more than to be let alone—to have things as they were before we came along.

One further report on rodents before we leave them: an experience I had while tenting in the Adirondacks. I referred to this little event in the first chapter; it provides an insight into the lives of wild animals—and into the imagination of campers, too.

Peg and I had turned in for the night in a remote section of those upstate New York mountains. The night was clear and warm, so we dispensed with the tent and merely unrolled our sleeping bags near a sheltering bank at the edge of a little-used wood road. We lay there in the dark, listening to the night sounds and glimpsing a star or two through the spruce canopy overhead. Then I drifted off to sleep.

I was awakened by something—I knew not what. Then I realized what had disturbed me: a tap on my backside as I lay curled in the sleeping bag. All was quiet, then the tap again. This time, however, it was more like a steady pressure. The pressure was released for a moment—only to be repeated.

I tried to think, there in the dark. No wind was blowing —it couldn't be spruce cones falling. Nor could it be a branch, swaying in the breeze. It was something active, animate—but what? What creature was cautiously—perhaps surreptitiously—probing around, back there where I couldn't see it? The tapping was odd enough—but why the occasional steady pressure? Was that unprotected portion of my anatomy being investigated for some reason? In fact, since nothing else made sense, was I being sized-up by some fearsome Creature, stealthily probing the right spot for a bite?

No sooner had this possibility presented itself than an answer began to form. After each tap, I suddenly realized, there was the slightest rustling in the leaves, perhaps four feet in front of me. Somehow the two were related—the tap and the sound.

Acting on a hunch, I slowly reached over toward the flashlight that lay by my head. Carefully twisting in my sleeping bag so I could view my nether region, I pressed the switch.

Sure enough, there was my Creature. As I pointed the flashlight behind me, a whitish object sailed into its gleam in a graceful arc. Landing on my stern, it vaulted off into the night. I heard it strike the leaves at the end of its second leap; then it bounded away once again. No sooner had it disappeared than a second apparition materialized and sprang away into the night.

Woodland jumping mice; that's what they were. Almost white in the gleam of the flashlight, the three-inch rodents were really light tan, with great long, fur-tipped tails nearly twice their length, that served to stabilize them in the air like the feathers of an arrow. Even in the uncertain light they were exquisite creatures, with tiny forepaws and powerful hind legs, like diminutive kangaroos.

I had unknowingly camped right in the pathway of these

playful rodents. They were using me as a springboard, jumping onto me from the nearby bank, off into the leaves —and back for another leap. The steady pressure, I realized, was when one of them paused a moment on the sleeping bag before continuing its rounds.

Once I had learned who the midnight revelers were, I merely had to move a short distance to be out of their trajectory. It may have ruined their night, but it sure helped mine.

One recurring fear held by campers has to do with another sort of visitor, who, supposedly, is lured to the sleeping bag almost like a moth to a flame. According to tradition and many a Hollywood Western, your preparations for the evening are observed in anticipation by those sinuous, sneaky scoundrels, the snakes. Then, just as you're curled up, along comes the serpent. In the movie it's always a poisonous one—seemingly big enough to swallow you, sleeping bag and all. Luckily, you spot it in time, and clobber it with a single magnificent shot in the dim light just as it coils to strike.

There is, indeed, a grain of truth to the story. Snakes, with little control over their own body heat, will seek a warm shelter on a chilly night. That warmth could be provided by a rock that has absorbed the sun's rays all day and now gives back the heat in the darkness. It could be provided by a strip of highway, acting like a great radiator, luring night creatures to bask there in the dark until they lose their lives beneath the wheels of a car. Indeed, Peg and I have rescued a number of rattlesnakes from just such a fate as their bodies lay stretched gratefully on the pavement during a chilly desert night.

The warmth may be offered by your cozy sleeping bag,

too. Offered, yes—but seldom accepted. Even when slumbering, you are much more active than a ribbon of roadway. A snake, with its exquisite sense of vibrations and its delicate forked tongue, which "licks" tiny odor particles from the air and transfers them to taste buds in the roof of its mouth, quickly discerns that you're no ordinary chunk of concrete.

Once such a revelation has occurred, the snake usually loses little time in a hasty escape. After all, its business in life is to keep *out* of danger. So the chance of a sleeping human and a wakeful reptile occupying the same patch of ground for even a few minutes are rare, indeed. If such an event should take place, it's due to no evil intent on the part of the reptile; it merely seeks to share a little warmth, that's all.

Incidentally, if you begrudge the snake even this amenity, you can load your own scales—in your favor. The majority of snakes make their living on the ground, so if you insist on sleeping without uninvited company, do your slumbering slightly higher than their level. The average trailer is all the insulation you need from a serpent in search of sociability. If you're in the jungle, a covered hammock slung between two trees is a fair guarantee you'll not be disturbed. A tent with floor and zip-up door will turn aside the most inquisitive reptile, too. Keep away from ledges, old stone walls, rocky wastelands: such spots are ideal haunts for mice and insects and, hence, for the snakes that search for them.

There's one other bit of insurance against snakes: The Law of Chance. I have yet to meet a camper who has played an unwitting Cleopatra and taken an asp to an involuntary bosom. Yet the fear exists, and those Western movies don't help a bit: snakes in the moonlight are great Box Office—even if they are apt to be *only* Box Office.

Getting to know a bit about them is also a help. I recall one time when a high school student brought me a whole gang of groggy garter snakes in a satchel. The snakes had been hibernating under a pile of lumber when he and a friend discovered them on a weekend exploration party. The boys captured an impressive number of the creatures: thirty-two of them, in fact. On Monday they brought them to biology class.

I had scheduled a series of laboratory periods for the week on osmosis, onion cells and other stimulating topics. Now, all at once, I had the chance to help a hundred-plus budding Vermonters to understand what their Green Mountain state was really all about. So I canceled the osmosis, took the onions home for Peg's hamburgers, and had an impromptu five days of lab on snakes.

The laboratory portion of biology divided my hundred students into five two-hour sections. These five sections met twice weekly, thus giving every student four lab hours a week. As the students spied the snakes, the first few minutes of each section bordered on consternation for some; shocked disbelief for others. Only a few in each class had ever been closer than a stone's throw—literally— to a snake.

"Here's your laboratory partner for the next two sessions," I told the incredulous sophomores as I reached into the large terrarium and extracted one of the captives. "You've got this whole week to learn all you can about snakes."

Aided by two of the more venturesome students, I placed a garter snake in each of twenty smaller terrariums

79

in front of the startled students. I sent a couple of helpers down to the library to get all the books they could bring back about snakes, and commissioned every student to do some outside reading before the next period. Books and pamphlets from my own shelves—plus the firsthand tutelage of the snakes themselves—would give an unparalleled acquaintance with reptiles in general, and snakes in particular.

It worked even better than I had hoped. Before the end of the week every one of those hundred students had actually held the gentle, inoffensive garter snakes. I jotted a few notes of their comments:

"Look, Bill—he presses right back when I touch him—just as if he *liked* to be petted."

"I always thought their tongue was a stinger. Why, it's so soft—it's softer than your eyelash!"

"Who says snakes are cold? This one's warmer than I am."

"Naw, Susie—it's not really *that* warm. It's just been lying in the sun, that's all."

"—And see how smooth it is. I used to think snakes were slimy, or icky, or something. But when I touch it, it's almost like—well, like stroking a bird."

There were a couple of anxious moments, I must admit. One of the snakes, perhaps resentful of being rousted out of its long winter sleep, promptly bit the first student who picked it up. Luckily the girl didn't panic, but just stood bravely while another girl disengaged the snake. The actual bite was next to nothing ("Heck, Mr. Rood, I've been scratched worse than that on a berry bush!") and a little first aid fixed her up in a couple of minutes.

The affair was a valuable lesson for the whole class: "Is

that all there is to a snakebite? What are we afraid of, then?"

Another uneasy moment occurred during the final session when one of the students came up to my desk at the start of a midmorning lab. "Mr. Rood," he said, "can I get a snake? Everybody else has one but me."

Sure enough, his glass terrarium was empty. I had checked at the end of the last class; all snakes had been accounted for. Somehow his specimen had pushed the top off the tank and had escaped.

I could just see the pandemonium if the missing snake turned up, say, in the English class down the hall. We immediately began an all-points search, checking the shelves, the drawers, the supply room. A couple of students helpfully invaded Paul Marshall's physics class next door and precipitated a gleeful time-out while eighteen seniors inspected desks, chairs—and even each other—in a hunt for the missing reptile.

Still no snake. Unwilling to trigger a general exodus of the whole school and break down all the good will I'd built up about snakes, I decided we'd better not borrow any more trouble. While the students were still hunting, I spirited one of the spare snakes from the big terrarium and casually deposited it near the sink. Then, hastily retiring to the microscope cabinet, I busied myself in a further search. Taking its cue perfectly, the garter snake waited a moment, then obligingly crawled out toward Mary Jackman, who hoisted it aloft in triumph.

The crisis was over. But the problem remained. It wasn't until almost a week later that it was solved. Merle Crown, the principal, sent a couple of boys up to me with a shoe box. Inside the box was the little wanderer; they'd found her near a radiator. She was dusty, dry and thirsty. I dunked her into a pan of water, where she swam for a moment and then lay still, working her jaws steadily as she drank for more than a minute.

We never learned how she had made her way along the hall, down the stairs, and across a corridor to the principal's office without being discovered—or being stepped on by milling students in the break between classes. But she was back in the laboratory and I was glad—even if, on her part, she might have preferred her winter lumber pile to the comfort of the classroom.

Perhaps I'd better explain my use of the feminine pronoun. How can you tell a female snake from a male, anyway? And, besides, who cares?

In case you wonder why anyone should bother, I have found that it's little questions like these—off on a tangent, as it were—that help apprehensive people to forget their fears for a moment. Sort of like the salesman who conveniently skirts the basic question of signing on the dotted line by asking his prospect "Do you wish to use your pen —or shall we use mine?"

Thus (and I'm taking you into that lab with me for the moment, where you remind yourself that your worries about snakes are not ingrown, but acquired), if you can concentrate on "sex" you may find yourself ignoring "snakes." Besides, you'll learn, as we did during that memorable week, how exquisitely the snake fits into its surroundings.

With its long, limbless body the snake has made a number of changes in its lifestyle. Not only must it move by forming itself into a series of S-curves and thrusting against tiny projections such as sticks and stones, but its other activities are unique, too. It detects your presence by feeling earth vibrations along its entire length, by noting movements with its ever-open, nearsighted eyes, and by constantly licking the air with its delicate tongue so as to transfer tiny odor particles to that tasting and smelling Organ of Jacobsen in the roof of its mouth.

It detects the opposite sex in much the same way. But, if you think of the normal course of events in the relation between the sexes, you might assume that the legless, armless snake was at a disadvantage when it came to the act of love.

Almost every creature has some device whereby one individual may clasp the other during mating: the embrace of many male amphibians that literally squeeze the eggs from the female, or the web with which some male spiders enshroud their fearsome mates to ensure that only one appetite at a time is satisfied. Male turtles have a convenient depression in the lower shell to fit the upper bulge of the female; the male angler fish applies himself so closely to the skin of his intended that his tissues actually graft themselves to hers. Insects have abdominal claspers; as they position themselves for mating, roosters literally snatch their mates baldheaded with their beaks. Even the quadrupeds such as horses and dogs employ their front legs to hold themselves in place. What, then, does a snake have?

Externally, if you look, there is apparently no difference between male and female. But look again. The vent (digestive-reproductive opening) of the female is well back along the underside, quite close to the tip of the tail. That of the male is much farther forward. And there, once you have interpreted what you see, is the difference between the sexes—and at least a partial answer to the question "what does a snake have to help him?"

Aided by a mutual twining of the two bodies, like the serpents in that familiar medical symbol the caduceus, and positioned exactly by that dextrous tail, the sexes can readily mate. A special arrangement of his sex organ, giving it a sort of double construction, allows this smooth-skinned male to couple with his smooth-skinned mate without once losing his place.

On the part of the female, having the vent quite near the tail gives a large space for her internal organs. Thus she has plenty of capacity to develop her eggs or, as with the garter snake and some others, to hold the eggs until they hatch in her body and her newborn young crawl forth.

This living laboratory was one of our most successful sessions of the year—one that a hundred students may never forget. In fact, it was so successful that, at the end of the week, all but a few snakes went home with their new-found friends. Doubtless when the reptiles got to their second homes the process of education started all over again.

During that week the inevitable question arose: what about poisonous snakes? What kinds are most common? Where do you find them—and how do you know one when you see it?

For our own state of Vermont—and for nearby upstate New York, plus southern Canada and northern New England—the answer is easy: your chances of meeting a poisonous snake are small, indeed. There are practically none at all in Maine, for instance. There are a few ledges and rockslides in remote areas where you still might meet a timber rattlesnake, but you'd better hurry if you want to find one. Most sightings of a rattler trigger a round of behavior that's little short of a lynching party. Sticks and stones go flying. A posse may hastily form if the unfortunate reptile escaped the first onslaught—and, soon, scratch one more rattlesnake

Rattlesnakes are easy to identify, if you can see the rattles. Other snakes, however, may vibrate the tail when agitated. If that tail happens to be in dry leaves, say, or against a resounding piece of wood, there's a "rattlesnake" that isn't. The only other poisonous snake that may work its way up into New England is the copperhead. It's a more southern species, however, and nearly every "copperhead" north of Connecticut (and they are rare, indeed, in that state, too) is probably the harmless milk snake—or checkered adder—about which more will be said in a moment. Water moccasins, coral snakes and diamondback rattlers are all more southern or western.

Generally, the nonpoisonous snakes hang on when they bite, thus making a ragged scratch. Poisonous snakes strike with wide-open mouth, stabbing with the two long fangs and quickly retreating. But analyzing the duration of chomp of a snake to see if its poisonous or not, is pretty late in the game for comfortable snake identification. The trouble is that there are no sure ways to spot poisonous snakes from a good long distance.

Get closer, however, and you can note the differences. Copperheads and rattlers (and water moccasins too) have a deep facial pit, larger than the nostril, in front of each eye on either side of the face; thus they are called pit vipers. The pits are exquisitely sensitive to animal heat, and enable their owner to find warmblooded prey. Then,

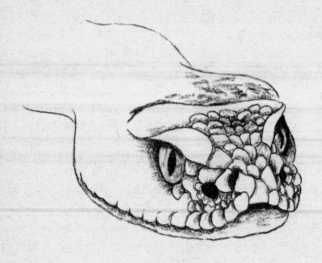

Pit Viper

too, the forward portion of the top of the head is predominately scaled in the pit vipers, while our northeastern nonpoisonous snakes have a large area of flat plates on the head. The eyes of pit vipers have slitlike pupils, like a cat, while those of our harmless northeastern snakes are round.

Still, it's a bit disconcerting to have to get down and look a snake in the eye. Better to learn them as individual species; there are only about fifteen of them, anyway, in our northeast.

A number of books will aid in identification, but it might be helpful to mention three special snakes here. These, all harmless, produce such a convincing demonstration of ferocity that more than one camp has been hastily struck because of dire peril from these "poisonous" creatures. All three may show markings that remind you of their venomous cousins. Then, again, their melanistic or dark phases may show no markings at all—which is also true for melanistic pit vipers.

The most common impostor on my own farm in north-central Vermont is the milk snake, or "checkered adder." Brown, black and white in a blotched pattern, the milk snake is often found around old barns and pasture fences. Supposedly it's there to steal milk from the cows; hence its name—although what self-respecting bossy would stand for such nonsense I have never figured out. Actually, the snake is a great mousetrap, as it can follow the mice down into their burrows. However, it defends itself vigorously when threatened and looks so like the brown-and-tan copperhead that every year I get two or three calls that begin: "There's this deadly-looking snake out in our yard, Mr. Rood. . . ."

Next in line is that sluggish-looking but alert sunbather, the eastern water snake. You can see it in almost any water east of the Rockies. Fat of body, with a triangular head and a wicked disposition when captured, the water snake looks like a deadly reptile for sure. "Water moccasins," we called them when I was a kid, even though the true moccasin would never venture north into our New England waters.

The presence of these creatures has caused needless worry to thousands of bathers. Swimming beaches have closed down because someone found a "moccasin." In reality the water snake is shy and harmless, and more afraid to swim with you than you are to swim with it—which, when I recall a frantic exodus of bathers at Connecticut's Black Rock Park when one was sighted, is a strong statement indeed.

The last member of the triumvirate is a born actor. Even if your only intention is to mind your own business, the hognose snake sees to it that you mind it somewhere else. Flattening its portly body and wheezing defiance, the "puff adder," as it's called, puts on a five-star display of histrionics—with the accent on the "hiss."

Stand and watch it for a while as it strikes horrendously in your direction. Refuse to be bullied, however, and *Heterodon contortrix* goes into the act that gives it the second part of its scientific name. Twisting and thrashing, the snake is rocked with spasms and convulsions. It is obviously in the last stages of a fatal seizure. One final gasp and its mouth drops open, ridiculous little forked tongue lolling out. It has just enough strength left to roll over on its back, like the mortally wounded cowboy who raises himself for that last avenging shot. And there is your puffing adder—dead.

Well, almost. Reach down and pick up its lifeless body. Gaze at the upturned nose; stroke the scaly skin and tell it how sorry you are that things came to this. Then put it down again—right side up. Slowly, resolutely, it twists until it's upside down. Right it once more, and it turns over again. Obviously, the only position for a dead snake is belly up.

Left to its own devices, the puff adder slowly recovers. Righting itself and testing the air with its tongue, it slinks away—if such a stout-bodied, snub-nosed spoofer could ever be accused of slinking. And with it, if you watched the whole performance, go your fears. They evaporated through understanding, just as can most dreads and apprehensions if you give them half a chance.

One further word about snakes before we go on to the

last of this chapter's purported rogues. There are plenty of books and manuals that tell about snakebite and its cure. Most physicians in high-bite areas now stock reserves of antivenin. You can stock your own supply of alcoholic "cure" if you desire, but better give it to the snake; it's well nigh worthless. In fact, it may dilate the blood vessels and cause trouble.

The best treatment still consists of keeping calm, constricting the blood flow back to the heart, making a small cut into each fang wound to induce bleeding and sucking the wound for half an hour. You don't need to worry about swallowing the venom: it's harmless when taken by mouth. And sores in your mouth will not absorb the poison, either your suction would draw material away from such sores rather than forcing it in.

It is a small step, at least in general appearance, from snakes to worms. Of course the similarity is more apparent than real, although worms have a couple of the characteristics often wrongly attributed to snakes: they're slimy and they're squishy. The fishermen and the gardener sing the praises of the lowly worm, while the rest of us may not be so enthusiastic.

Actually, just as is the snake—or any other animal—the worm is marvelously fitted for the kind of life it leads. If it were not so adapted it would soon yield to the fierce competition that exists even in the soil.

The earthworm's food consists largely of organic matter. Occasionally, as it stretches out on a lawn after a rain, it can find an ancient leaf that may serve as a banquet for several days. Maneuvering the leaf around with a prehensile lip, the worm pulls its prize down the hole, stem first. Sometimes this is more than a one-night job and, if you look, you may find leaves in various stages of migration into wormholes where the little harvesting operations were called on account of daylight.

Most of the worm's lifetime, however, is spent hidden in the soil. Here is where it helps to be flexible and stream-lined—and slippery. There is much organic matter in the soil: decaying roots, humus, fragments of soil animals. To sort them out from unyielding mineral fragments would involve a major sifting operation, so the worm adopts a magnificent shortcut. It merely takes everything into its body: sand grains, organic matter and all. It does this by opening its mouth over and over, swallowing its way through the soil. The slime on its skin serves to grease the skids, while its flexible body negotiates around pebbles and other obstacles with ease.

The soil, remaining relatively in place as the worm encompasses it, receives a charge of digestive fluid and a thorough kneading in the creature's body. The organic material is absorbed by this miniature mixmaster, while the indigestibles are left behind as lumps of debris known as castings. These castings, rich in food waste, act as tiny pats of fertilizer, nourishing the soil. As many as ten thousand castings have been counted on an acre of ground—and there are thousands more beneath the surface.

To look at an earthworm, stretching there in your freshly turned garden, you'd hardly suspect such an intriguing way of getting a living. Nor would you dream that the rubbery little creature actually shows a smattering of intelligence. Impossible as it may seem, a worm can be taught to run a simple Y-shaped course, picking right from left at the junction of the "Y." Choosing the proper arm of the "Y," it gets a reward of nice, cool earth. On the other hand, there's the discomfort of dry sand or a mild shock if it makes the wrong choice. That nondescript critter, apparently hardly knowing the difference between its head and its tail (but, of course, it does), is actually capable of making a decision.

There are many more strings to the earthworm's bow. Indeed, scientists feel that if man stands at the height of complexity and the lowly amoeba stands near the other extreme, the earthworm would be placed just about in the middle. It can "see," for instance, although it has no eyes —as many a fisherman has discovered when he tried to pick earthworms off the lawn at night with the aid of a flashlight. It can "hear" without ears as it receives vibrations in the soil. It has a tiny brain, several pumping organs, and even vessels filled with red blood. Not only that, but each mature earthworm has the complete reproductive organs of both sexes in a single individual. So, I guess, you'd say it is not an "it" at all: it is a "them."

Doubtless this quick explanation of the workings of an earthworm will not decrease its sliminess one bit, nor make it any less wiggly if you're squeamish. But with understanding comes caring—so, nod with new respect as you drape it on the hook and send it out into that pool after the Big One.

Poking along, last in line, is a being that would seem to have no redeeming features at all. Indeed, it appears to have no features of any kind. This nonentity is the almost-formless freeloader among your lettuce and flowers: the common slug.

A slug is, briefly, a snail without a shell. Occasionally it bears a shell of sorts within its body: a bit of gristle that's about as useful as a deflated tire. Most of the time, however, its only apology for a shell is a pad of soft tissue that seems to ride its back like a saddle. Yet the slug is not

Slug

without protection; the thousands that cross the sidewalks and climb on the grass and help themselves to your garden are proof that there's something in their favor.

The answer is found in their most outstanding attribute: that slimy coat. A slug spends its entire lifetime within an envelope of mucus. The gunky material serves to protect the body against drying. It forms a gluey mess that discourages predators. Sometimes it may contain a poison, as well: once I fed some woodland slugs to a dozen trusting frogs I'd raised for two months in the laboratory: within twelve hours the frogs were dead.

Mucus is not only a way of life for the slug; it's a way of travel, as well. Laying down a pathway of the slippery material, the slug glides over it like a tractor on an endless tread. Scratchy sand, thirsty concrete, even a jumble of dry lawn clippings are but a highway to the slug, which takes them all in its never-ending stride. One of the most impressive accomplishments of all is the ability of this soft-bodied mollusc to glide lengthwise on a razorblade without slicing itself in two.

Formless as it may seem, the soft body of the slug contains most of the organs that we possess. It can boast a liver, a heart, a single kidney. Like its shelled cousins, it has a pair of eyes—complete with lens, cornea and retina —borne aloft by two tentacles. A rasping, filelike tongue scrapes samples of cabbage or clover or any convenient food as it glides along. It even rasps away at dead animals or other disposables, thus doing service as a scavenger. It has a pair of organs of balance, too, so it can tell upside from down—for what such information may be worth to a slug.

Like the earthworm, many slugs have both sexes in a single individual. A mutual exchange of sperm takes place when two likeminded slugs get together. Soon a cluster of eggs, like miniature grapes, is deposited under a stone— surrounded, of course, by the ever-present mucus.

Such a thumbnail sketch probably would do little toward endearing slugs to anybody. Nor, as I've said before, do these pages try to make the cast of characters a lovable assortment. But, at least, the critters have had their day in court, so to speak.

No. From mice to molluscs, they've scuttled and slunk before you and, perhaps left you singularly unimpressed. However, I have one final comment:

Just how, I wonder, does the parade of padded, per-fumed, tranquilized, transistorized, hurrying humans appear to *them*?

5 · Flyers and Flappers

There you are, right in the middle of it. A brown creature flutters past as you hastily duck deeper into the chair.
It flies over to the far corner of the room and makes a big
circle. Then it swings back and heads straight for you.

That settles it. You cringe to avoid a direct hit, catapult
yourself out of your seat, and leave the room in a running
crouch as if you were under sniper fire.

The cause of such an exodus is one of the world's most
maligned and misunderstood creatures: the bat. And small
wonder that you're startled; for as far as we humans are
concerned, there's practically nothing to recommend such
a critter. The pushed-in bulldoglike features, eyes seem-
ing too small for its face, and ears crinkled and deformed
make it appear like something out of science fiction. Its
zigzag, erratic flight is jerky and disconcerting—a sort of
airborne scuttle, like a rodent with wings. Hence, the
German *der Fledermaus*: the flitter-mouse.

Then, too, the bat flies at night. Such behavior makes it
highly suspect, right there. Any critter with nothing to

hide would go around in the daylight like a fine, upright human being. Since it performs best under cover of darkness the bat *must* be up to no good. It carries diseases, for instance. It drifts down when you're asleep, attacks you, and drinks your blood. And if you are topped with an enthusiastic crop of hair, better watch out—the bat might fly right into it.

Folktales, all of them. Or are they? Just how many stories about bats can you believe?

Well, like a lot of such tales, there's a grain of truth somewhere. There are, indeed, vampire bats abroad on business that's less than commendable—from our standpoint, at least, although it is fine from theirs. Bats have been found to carry disease, too, and they have even been known to tangle in people's hair.

Of course, such undignified behavior as that last item is entirely unscheduled; the bat would rather it didn't happen, either. And, in our haste to escape the neighborhood frequented by a bat, we neglect the other side of the story—the tremendous value of these little fly-by-nights.

Before trying to assure you that you're glad there's a bat or two sharing your existence, let's take a quick look at the darker side. To find a vampire, for example, you'd have to travel to the tropics. Apparently, potential victims —human and animal—dress too warmly to attract the vampire bat to cooler regions; thus the tender portions of the victim's anatomy are less exposed than in tropical climates. Then, too, perhaps the vampires just cannot take the cold weather. Whatever the reason for the omission, the razor-toothed little mammal that nicks your skin and then laps the ensuing trickle of blood will be one worry that need not bother you. If, somehow, you *should* find yourself in vampire haunts, the possible damage you'd sustain is not much worse than if you'd knocked a knuckle on the knob of a door. Besides, there has to be some compensation meted out to you for leaving the rest of us to cope with winter, anyway.

Another fear is that of potential spread of disease by bats. Every summer, it seems, there's an item in the newspaper about these animals as carriers of rabies. Somebody noticed a bat acting strangely; he captured it, sent it to the laboratory, and the results came back positive. We've had rabid bats in New England and scientists have found them in other parts of the country, too. One of Peg's kindergarten children discovered a bat one morning, got nipped when she tried to pick it up, and had to undergo a precautionary series of rabies shots because the bat escaped before it could be tested.

The possibility of rabies is there, apparently, in any warmblooded animal that acts strangely. There have been rabid dogs, rabid cats, skunks, foxes—even rabid cows—found in the throes of the disease and, usually, put out of their misery.

The whole point about these unfortunate creatures is that they act strangely. They stagger, fall, run, attack other animals. Bats show special symptoms, too: stupor, dizzyness, inability to fly. Normal behavior—that is, as normal as all that zooming and diving and reversing can seem to us—most probably indicates a normal bat.

As for getting into your hair—well, why not? At least, under the circumstances where it's been known to happen. A bat indoors is scarcely able to negotiate freely. Those high-pitched squeaks it makes to find its way and locate its food must bounce off the walls in a confusing pattern.

Ordinarily it can tell by the echo where there is a moth, a building, a tree. However, a couple of humans in a room, flailing around with arms or brooms or folded newspapers are more than it bargained on, and wildly waving hair just might get in the way of a wildly flying bat.

If you merely let it explore, the bat will often leave the room by the same route it entered. That echo location is marvelously sensitive, and quickly tells the little mammal of an open door or window, or even a hole in the wall. One team of scientists trapped several dozen bats in a cave by stretching a fine-mesh net over the cave's opening. When they went back later to count the captives, there were no captives: the bats, with their delicate sonar, had cruised back and forth along the mesh of the net until they had located a spot where a few strands had broken. Landing at the hole, they crawled out, one by one, and escaped.

That delicate hearing goes hand in hand with split-second timing. Most of those zany twists and turns negotiated by a bat are the result of its reaction to echoes of insects in the air. Those staccato squeaks bounce off a moth, say, and the bat turns aside for an airborne snack. Toss a pebble at it and the bat turns aside, too—but only for an instant. Something in the echo says "fake!" and the bat zooms away just before contact. Fly fishermen sometimes catch bats with their hooks—but almost always in the wing or body. The little animals swerve toward the lure, size it up as an imitation, and veer away. They cannot reckon on the fishline, however; the filament whips around a wing or leg, snaring them.

It's that intentness on everything in the air that makes our bats so valuable. They're marvelous insect traps. Let a swarm of mosquitoes join you at an evening picnic, say, and the bats may be there, too. Coursing back and forth, almost as if swinging on an unseen pendulum, they snatch those pesky skeeters, one after another. High-speed photographs show that, if a bat misses an insect with its mouth, it may alter its flight just a bit, reach out with a wingtip or the web between its hind legs, and still scoop it in. So the flight of the flitter-mouse, haphazard as it looks, is precise indeed.

With such an active life, the domestic portion of the bat's existence has a slant of its own. Mother bat may be away most of the night—a long time for her nursing youngster to be without food. So the baby goes right along with her as soon as he's old enough to cling to her fur. She pursues her prey there in the dark, a bit labored because of the added weight, but still able to catch a night's meal. It must be quite an exhilarating childhood for the little fellow. Finally, when he's too much of a burden, she sends him off on his own.

A friend of mine took a swipe with a broom at a bat. She managed to connect, whereupon the bat split in two. Apparently it was a mother toting an adolescent youngster, who thereby got his flying papers faster than planned. Or perhaps she'd uncoupled a mating pair; they often travel like this at such times.

There are other fliers abroad at night besides the bats. Owls drift through the woods and over the meadows like great, silent moths. Nighthawks cruise back and forth high over a city, where they gorge on insects attracted by the lights. Their white-spotted wings and nasal "peent" in flight make them familiar to many a city boy who hardly knows a robin. Their relatives the whippoorwills and chuck-will's-widows join the night life, too, but out in the country.

You'll probably never see nighthawks closer than those

brief glimpses overhead, and their country cousins seem little more than monotonous but pleasant calls in the dark, either. Their shadowy neighbors, the owls, are something else again. The owls' mournful cries may burst on you at any time, and the thought of the great birds out there in the night, sharpening their beaks and talons, can lend more than a little spice to an evening stroll.

A man I know was walking along an overgrown path just at dusk. The bushes were almost head high, and he had to push his way through them, sometimes only guessing at the trail. His straw hat was pulled down to shelter his face against the whipping branches.

All at once there was a rush of wings—and his hat sailed off into the night. An owl—perhaps the great horned owl, which is large enough for such a feat—had spotted the hat bobbing along and has swooped down after this bush-top "rabbit."

Only where the man was hidden would the owl make such a mistake, however. Normally an owl's senses tell it all about you and it drifts away so you never know it has been there. Not only are its huge eyes capable of seeing in the dimmest light, but its ears are among the keenest in the bird world.

Consider the face of an owl for a moment. Each great eye is set in a shallow disc of feathers. The two discs overlap in the beak area so the owl appears to have a flattened face. At the outer edge of each disc are hidden auditory openings located in such a way that the discs serve to focus the sounds, just as you'd cup your ear to catch a faint noise.

Nor is that all: the owl's eyes, in the center of those discs, are immovable. Thus, wherever it looks, its sharpest focus is precisely where the ears are listening, too. By turning its head the slightest fraction, the owl thus brings its two keenest sense to bear on a faint rustling in the leaves or some tiny motion on the ground.

Nor is *that* all, either. In order not to interfere with its own hearing or to warn the prey of its approach, the owl is clothed in soundproofed plumage. The outer edges of its feathers are soft and downy, thus eliminating any telltale whistle as it dives. The sum total of it all is a gifted creature able to find and capture its prey on the darkest night. In fact, in one laboratory experiment a tame owl, placed in a totally dark room, easily caught a fuzzy "mouse" resting in shredded newspapers and given the slightest twitch with a string.

No, the wise old owl is well aware of what it is about. You need never fear that you'll be mistaken for a mouse or a rabbit, at least from the owl's point of view. Of course, if you wander through dense bushes with a white straw hat—or, I suppose, a ravishing blond wig—you're on your own.

The gentleman got his hat back, by the way. He found it the following day on top of a bush—right where the disgusted owl had dropped it.

Those daytime marauders, the hawks, are masters in their chosen realm, as well. The eyesight of some hawks has been measured to be eight times as keen as ours. Some hawks go even further and have two points of focus in each eye, rather than the one that we possess. In addition, many of them have true binocular vision, giving a depth of field that allows them to strike with pinpoint accuracy. And when, as in the rare peregrine falcon, you're in a hurtling dive that may reach a hundred fifty miles per hour, you'd better be precise about your depth perception or you'll spread yourself over half an acre.

Fierce as these creatures may be with their telescopic sights, hooked beaks and "big, fanged feet," to quote one of my biology students, the chance they'd ever attack you is just about zero. Even when its young are threatened, a hawk will usually stop short of actually using its beak and claws to rake an intruder. However, the sight and sound of an outraged predatory bird, hooked bill open in a scream, zooming in one wings that may spread as wide as six feet in eagles and ospreys, must give the shivers to many a would-be nest thief.

The least attractive of the flesh-eating birds are those homely-looking creatures, the vultures. With their naked heads, hooked beaks, black wings so long that they look like a cloak when folded—these birds would scarcely win a beauty prize. But that's from our point of view. From their standpoint, they are adapted to their work as scavengers as perfectly as a butterfly fits a sunny meadow. Far from being an object of scorn and dread, the vulture should receive our grateful—if grudging—admiration.

Once again, everything fits. The vulture's great wings give it tremendous lift and soaring capacity. The greatest wingspan among land birds—eleven feet—is shared by two vultures, the California condor and its close cousin the Andean condor. Only one other bird, the magnificent giant albatross—itself a master at soaring for days over the ocean—has an equal wingspan. Such a great spread of wing is necessary for the vultures' method of finding food: drifting above the earth for hours while searching the ground for carrion.

In its circling, each vulture keeps an eye on others of its

kind. That female, soaring over Sunny Valley, has dropped lower; perhaps she sees something—so her neighbor glides over from half a mile away to investigate. Seeing him change position, three more vultures drift toward the spot, as well. They are imitated by others—and the whole pattern of vultures in the sky converges toward Sunny Valley. It's as if a great unseen net in the sky were pulled downward at the point occupied by that female, with tightening and funneling of its invisible "mesh" as a result.

If it's only a false alarm, the female rises again and the net relaxes to its original position. If it's a potential meal, however, she descends to a nearby tree to wait for sun and decomposition to soften the carcass. Her neighbors—and their neighbors, and theirs—fly to the scene. They come from so far away that humans, watching, feel sure that the distant birds must have smelled the feast; they couldn't possibly have seen it, down in the bushes and two mountain ranges away.

When the vultures begin to feed, the reason for the naked head and neck becomes apparent. Decaying food may be soft and mushy; it would create a problem as it caked on the feathers. A featherless head means a neater bird even if, to us, it seems unattractive. But vultures—or hyenas, or crocodiles or any other unlovely creatures you may think of—were hardly put on earth for our delight. They are shaped and colored and constructed for business of their own.

Few other birds than the predatory birds seem to be cause for concern to most of us. True, we hurl invectives at a messy flock of starlings, or rig a framework with a hat and coat in a cornfield to scare the crows. However—with the exception of those cedar waxwings that frightened me as a tot, and some bird that may have caught you unawares, as well—most people can get along with most birds most of the time. In fact, the birding fraternity tells us, nearly one out of two persons in the United States and Canada has a feathered friend—either in a cage, on a dooryard feeder or down at the city park.

The air is populated by more than bats and birds, how ever. Indeed, scientists tell us, these furried and feathered aviators are mere upstarts compared to the oldest flyers of them all: and here we are, back with the insects again.

Just a page or two about them, this time, despite their venerable half-a-billion-year history. The day of the twenty-inch dragonfly faltered with that of the foot-long cockroach, long before the occurrence of bizarre leather-winged prebirds or the first tiny mammals that dug up the dinosaur eggs and hastened the doom of those great reptiles. Today's dragonflies, for instance, are of a more manageable size: six inches long in jumbo species, with conventional forms half that length.

Thus far in this book I've had to admit that, here and there, you may be in for trouble following too close an acquaintance with certain of its characters. With dragonflies, however, you can rest easy. In spite of their names of darning needles and devil doctors, they will do you no harm.

Why, then, do they have such a fearsome reputation? Because, as in nearly every creature that gives us pause, we labor under half-truths and misunderstandings about them. Even the common name—dragonfly—conjures up a picture of a monster.

"Keep away from the swamp," my grandmother used to warn Irma and Jimmy and me. "The darning needles will sew up your ears." In Africa they are supposed to sew up your lips, or even your eyelids. And in South America, you had better stay clear of those devil doctors: they'll sting you half to death.

Actually darting back and forth, back and forth over a pond or meadow, the dragonfly is a living insect trap. Its six legs, bunched together on its thorax, are set with bristly hairs and spines. As it flies, it holds the spiny legs so as to make a basket. Great compound eyes of as many as a thousand facets each spot the tiniest gnat. The hapless creature is scooped into that fatal basket—and the dragonfly has just lived up to its name. Passing the gnats and mosquitoes forward to busy jaws, the arrow-shaped predator is forever eating, like a boy munching a candy bar as he walks down the street.

Dragonflies, seeking out their prey in such precise fashion, are far better than any manmade insecticide. Unfortunately, they succumb to many of the chemicals that lay other insects low, so when you spray the mosquitoes, you also knock the dragonflies for a loop.

A few years ago the town fathers of a coastal Virginia community had to trim the budget. Roads needed all the money they could get; so did schools and other essentials, so the axe fell on mosquito control. The fogging trucks stayed in their garages and the spray rigs lay idle all that summer. Sure enough, the skeeters rolled in almost like a dust cloud over a desert.

Peg and I happened to be on a photography trip in the marshes that summer, and the mosquitoes were fierce. But on a certain island we saw Phase One of natural control getting under way: hundreds of reddish dragonflies, searching back and forth over the grasstops in deadly squadrons, their wings rustling as they cleared the marsh of thousands of the biting little pests.

Since it takes a while for predators to build up in response to an increase in their prey, however, Phase Two —the general burgeoning of dragonflies and other insect enemies of mosquitoes—never had the chance to occur. The mosquito explosion alarmed the taxpayers into a resounding bulge in the budget. Now the mosquito level is down again; but, then, there are none of those fearsome devil's darning needles, either.

Another winged insect that has frightened taxpayers out of their pocketbooks is the one that appears by the thousands from holes in the ground in spring and summer. The winged reproductive forms of termites sometimes take to the air in clouds. I have seen colonies of them so thick that, at a distance, they look like a wisp of smoke. "Flying ants," they are often called, and they are done to death in droves by birds, lizards, dragonflies and their human neighbors.

You can tell a true termite from a true ant by a glance at its middle. Genuine ants, being relatives of the wasps, have the typical slender wasp waist. Termites are thick-bodied throughout, whether they are the dark-colored, airborne explorers out to find some new house to undermine, or the wingless white workers who stay behind and accomplish the same result at home.

It helps your own woodwork not at all to destroy the winged forms. They're concerned only with carrying the delights of their kind to new regions. In their explorations they will leave their present nest far behind. Mating together, a male and female termite descend to earth at some fresh un-termite-blessed spot. She explores until she finds just the right combination of tasty wood and moisture; an old stump, perhaps, or the sills of a house in contact with the ground. Her mate trots after her until, finding the right spot, they chew out a little cave for themselves and set up housekeeping.

Termite, winged stage

This may be the last that is seen of them, or their many resulting wingless progeny, for years—or until the floor caves in. The mated pair may live as many as forty years in some termite species, thus giving them the longest life-span among insects. Their sharp-jawed descendents nip away at the timbers, carefully leaving the external layers intact. If, as they chew, the wood fibers break with too much of a snap, they no longer excavate in that region: the snap indicates a strain. Hence an entire building may be rendered a hollow shell while appearing as sound as ever.

One band of termites chewed up through the floor of a little-used home. Happening to strike the leg of a piano, they proceeded up through the rest of the instrument. After they had been at work several months, some tenants moved into the home. The new lady of the house sat down to play the piano. No sooner had she struck the first chord than a string popped. This threw the strain on other parts of the sounding board and more strings gave way. In another instant the piano roared in pain, belched a great cloud of dust, and settled to the floor with a sigh.

This chain reaction took place in the Deep South— Louisiana, to be exact. Termites are seldom a serious problem in the northern states and Canada. The cold, apparently, is too much for them. I once pointed this happy circumstance out to a hard-bitten Vermont neighbor of mine. "Now I know," he said, wanly, "why I'm living here. I knew there must be *some* reason to stay in all this snow and ice."

Northern regions do not have termites to any extent, it is true. Genuine flying ants, however, burst from the ground, periodically, during the summer. They are usually no cause for alarm, as they live harmlessly in the soil. Carpenter ants, those large black creatures sometimes half an inch long, live in galleries in the wood, like termites, but they excavate only for their living quarters. Termites actually consume the wood as nourishment.

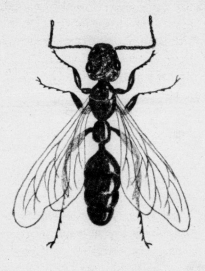

Flying Ant

When a newly fertilized queen ant drops to earth after her wedding flight, she has to begin her colony all by herself. Her spouse, dying soon after mating, drops away, and she is left alone. Breaking off the now-useless wings, she burrows into the earth, where she constructs a tiny chamber. Here, nourished by slow absorption of the large wing muscles, she cares for her first few eggs.

The tiny ant larvae receive a minimum of food. Their meager rations are passed to them from the queen's own stomach. The larvae transform into tiny ants known as minims. Now, at last, there are workers to help the queen. They make their way to the outer world, where they forage for food to feed their mother. She lays more eggs, and soon the colony is under way. The queen mother, however, stays in the dark: those brief few minutes of her mating flight were the only sunlight she would ever see.

Another creature of darkness is that legendary Rip van Winkle, the seventeen-year "locust," or periodical cicada. We lived on Long Island one year when these large insects appeared by the millions. They'd been hidden in the soil in the nymph stage for seventeen years, feeding on the sap of roots Then, following some unknown signal during the last of May, they poked their way out of the ground over much of the Island's south shore. Each nymph emerging from the soil left a hole the size of a dime.

The cicada's story is a remarkable one. Climbing upward, the nymph reaches a point where it can cling firmly to a support. There the brown, humpbacked creature rests and waits. Soon a split appears along its back. The skin ruptures and a new insect crawls out: gauzy-winged, ruby-eyed, brown and looking a bit like a huge housefly as big as the last joint of your index finger.

The wings dry and the insect begins its song. High-pitched and intermittent at first, it finally goes on without ceasing, as these giant cousins of the common aphids—or plant lice—pour all seventeen years of silence and darkness into their week in the sun.

The vocalizing is left to the males; the females will play their role in the next few days. Both sexes fly about, however. They fall into puddles, zoom around streetlights, land on pets and people: a veritable plague of buzzing "locusts."

After mating the female climbs or flies to a slender twig. There she jabs its growing tissues with her ovipositor. She inserts several dozen eggs into the resulting slits. The eggs hatch into tiny, antlike nymphs which scamper about for a few days and then disappear into the ground for seventeen more years.

A while ago the locusts appeared again on Long Island. Seventeen years have passed since I first saw them. Their numbers, although enough to excite the newspapers, were fewer; whole acres of them were covered by parking lots, or excavated to build new homes. In another seventeen years, doubtless, there will be less of them still.

These cicadas (they are not "locusts," for the latter are a type of grasshopper) have caused dread and consternation during their infrequent appearances. A certain pattern of veins in the wing forms a dark letter "W"—which, according to early soothsayers, stood for War. Like many superstitions, it carried a smattering of truth: wars seem to occur about once a generation or, roughly, every seventeen years.

In truth, of course, the "W" is but a coincidence. Nor can the large insects, for all their dagger-shaped ovipositors or piercing beaks, do any real damage. They suck very little plant sap during those few days of excitement, and even the twigs that are weakened by the insects' egg-laying are soon replaced. But, as there are several "crops" of these cicadas staggered over differing cycles in various parts of the country, a new "locust" scare hits the headlines every few years.

Last of the flyers on this list—although you doubtless could add a few of your own—is a familiar bit of local nighttime color. There you are, sitting quietly on a spring evening, when there's a buzz like a tiny lawnmower coming your way. Sailing toward the electric light comes an Unidentified Flying Object the size of a grape.

There's a thud as the Thing crashes full tilt into the light. Staggering from the impact, it catches itself in mid-air, swings around in a banking turn, and zeros in for another crack.

This time it's not so lucky. Stalled out completely, it drops to the floor. There it lies ignominiously on its back, legs waving helplessly: the shiny brown bungler known as the May beetle.

Unless it can grab hold of something to help right itself, the beetle may be doomed on the flat surface. In the soil where it lived as a big grub surrounded by delicious roots, or in the natural world of tasty leaves and flowers on a spring night, the "June bug" can hardly be expected to learn to cope with a smooth floor. It was your light that wooed it off course in the first place and, often, it is only your intervention that will make things right again.

May Beetle or June Bug

Reach down and it clings to you with as many of its clawed feet as possible Carefully disengage the clumsy creature and toss it into the air after turning off the light to rectify your wrong. Away goes the May beetle, gratefully humming a tune of thanks.

Now, turn on the lamp again. But, this time, close the screen. Or go indoors. Or just sit there and enjoy the dark. Do something, at any rate; that bright light will call the insects, and the insects will call the bats. And you don't want to take a chance on rabies and vampires and bats in your hair, now, do you?

6 · ...And Waterborne Wigglers

Can toads give you warts? They sure can; but only if you're a tadpole—in which case you'll inherit them.

Otherwise, you're wart-free—at least from the standpoint of these lumpy amphibians. Swim right in the same water where, just a few weeks ago, the toads sang their evening trills and draped their thousands of eggs in long strings on subsurface sticks and weeds. Or take a plunge right among the myriad black wriggling youngsters, if you like; you may scare the tadpoles half to death, but you'll emerge with nary an added blemish.

Nor do you need to worry about waffle-skinned old sobersides as he squats among the clods of earth in your garden and wreaks havoc among the insects; he'll keep his warts entirely to himself. They make fine camouflage. In addition, a couple of large lumps just behind the eyes contain a distasteful fluid that turns potential enemies away after they take an experimental bite. Many cats and dogs will ignore toads completely; they've had a sample, thanks, and that was enough.

True, a few toads have a genuine venom in those two parotid glands above the neck region—if a toad could be said to have a neck. In fact, the milky fluid squeezed from these glands in some tropical toads is used as a poison for darts and arrows. However, the toads—and frogs, for that matter—of our temperate zones lack such lethal refinements. Washing your hands after picking them up will be all the precaution you need; not for warts, of course, but to rinse away any bitter taste.

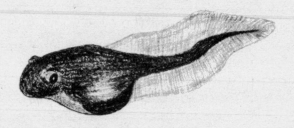

Tadpole or Poliwog

Those tadpoles (or, if you prefer, polliwogs) have no potential for harm, either. Their few weeks in the water are spent gleaning algae and other edibles from rocks and bottom debris with scrub-brush lips and vacuum-cleaner mouths. In spite of their harmlessness, however, the tadpoles in their numbers have given an anxious time at many a summer camp or resort. Nearly every year, I get a phone call or two from some worried waterfront director who has visions of the beach being closed because of "all those little black wigglers right along the edge of the shore, Mr. Rood."

Often the fear of tadpoles is not for what they are but for what they might be. After they have absorbed their yolk sac, new-formed tadpoles are about a quarter-inch long, black, and ribbonlike. They swim with a rippling motion, like a tiny snake in the water, giving rise to thoughts of eels and leeches. Then, soon, my telephone rings.

Actually, the clue to whether you have a tadpole or not lies partly in its name. The term "tadpole" hearkens back to two Middle English words: *tadde* (toad) and *pol* (head)—making this "the toad head" (the legs come later when the tail is absorbed). The parentage of "polliwog" is practically perfect: "pol" and "wygle" (wiggle)—which portrays a polliwog precisely.

Soon the "head that wiggles" grows into its typical shape and the camp officials breathe more easily. On occasion, however, they do come up with a genuine leech or baby eel. A bona fide leech may be a cause for some concern; a true baby eel, never.

Leeches, or bloodsuckers, have had their share of notoriety. In the tropics there are forms that live on land, but most North American leeches live in the water. Here, again, if you can put aside the shivers long enough, you find a creature that fits perfectly into its chosen life. In fact, an anticoagulant produced by the lowly leech may have fitted into *your* life already—and you were glad of it. Because their saliva contains a substance known as hirudin, which, when mixed with blood, retards coagulation in that area, it is used in surgery.

A word, first, about leeches in general. Related to the earthworm, a leech is able to expand and contract, much like its soil-dwelling cousin. However, earthworms have tiny bristles that can be poked out through their slippery coating to make them nonskid at will as they travel along through the soil. The leech, on the other hand, has only a tough, smooth skin. Instead of bristles it makes use of two suckers, one at either end of the body. Aided by these it alternately loops and extends itself, traveling along like an inchworm. Or, releasing both suckers, it swims through the water with undulations that are among the most graceful in nature.

Swimming with such ease is only one of its accomplishments. The arrangement of muscles in a leech can stretch it out to more than eight inches in larger specimens, or contract it into a tough little ball. It often takes the latter pose when waiting for a suitable meal. Inactive as it may seem, it is constantly sampling every change in the water about it.

The leech easily detects the faintest odor of a passing fish or salamander. Alert to changes in pressure and the eddies that precede a moving body in the water, it gauges the direction and speed of an approaching turtle or water beetle—and skillfully intercepts its victim. Even a sudden shadow will cause it to stretch out inquiringly, and its sense of smell is so keen that you can rub your finger on the inside of a dish, fill the dish with water, drop in a leech—and it will carefully explore that invisible fingerprint.

Within a leech's forward sucker are tough little jaws with sharp, cutting edges. If the leech finds a snail or tadpole—or your bare leg as you wade through the water—it quickly attaches, swings its body around until it finds just the right spot, and takes a nip. Then it injects the substance, hirudin, into the bloodstream to prevent clotting of the blood in the area where it is feeding.

What does the bite of a leech feel like, anyway? Well,

it is about like an underwater mosquito. I have been bitten on a number of occasions—and seldom even knew it at the time. That anticoagulant saliva supplied by the leech may give a local itching, but nearly all the saliva is drained back out again in the process of feeding.

If you discover you're providing lunch for a leech, chances are you'll take sudden steps to terminate the arrangement. Then, to your dismay, you discover that the slight wound continues to bleed. The hirudin keeps on working, preventing clotting for several minutes. But that is about all the danger there is from the attention of a bloodsucker—unless you happen to be a hemophiliac, or "bleeder." The free-flowing wound quickly cleans itself.

The term "leech" once applied to physicians who were engaged to let out your bad blood when you were sick. As recently as Grandpa's day, you could rent a medicinal leech from the local pharmacist. Then you could apply it to a black eye or a bruise. Kept moist with a light compress, the creature obligingly reduced your pain and swelling.

I recall standing as a boy before a whole jarful of the green and brown critters in the drugstore in Terryville, Connecticut. I could not understand why they rented them out when I could get ones that looked about the same in Scopino's Pond—now rechristened as a lake with a glamorous name. Lest the Lake Association cry "foul," however, I hasten to certify that I haven't found a leech there in years.

Black eyes and bruises are seldom ministered to by do-it-yourself leeches these days. That hirudin, however, has found still another use. Obtained from mouth glands of certain leeches, it may be employed as an anticoagulant, preventing dangerous clots in the bloodstream. I suspect the price of application is higher than in my boyhood, too. As I recall, the sign on that jar in the drugstore indicated you could have a day and a night with any leech of your choice for a quarter.

There are about half a hundred American leech species, the smallest of which could resemble the newborn tadpoles that started this chapter. They often occupy the same water, too, thus being scattered over most of our continent excepting the northernmost regions.

To jump from a four-inch leech to a four-foot eel may seem quite a leap, but the step to a baby eel is less fanciful. Small eels, called elvers, may be mistaken for leeches at first glance, as they swim with much the same sinuous motion. However, eels have a fishlike head, gills and forward fins. The rest of the eel stretches out into that disconcertingly snaky body.

Baby eels hatch out as tiny, flat, transparent creatures. All North American freshwater eels begin their lives in the Sargasso Sea, near Bermuda. Drifting and swimming toward the coast for a year, they gradually assume the familiar eel shape. The three-inch male elvers remain near the mouths of rivers, but the females propel themselves upstream like little salmon. Unable to ascend a waterfall, they may go around the obstacle on a rainy night, slithering uphill through the wet grass until they get above the falls.

Up they go, taking weeks, months—even years—in a series of short stays in several ponds, until each one finally arrives in Paradise Lake, or wherever her last stop may be. There, one summer day, you and she happen to meet. Swimming harmlessly along over the bottom, she takes the wrong turn and glides right past your bare feet.

You flounder ashore in a panic. The frightened creature

retreats into the depths, and your Paradise Lake has just become Paradise Lost. For no amount of money will you enter *that* water again.

Actually, no matter how serpentine it may appear, that eel is more closely related to a trout, say, or to a minnow than it is to a snake. Eels are fish; simple as that. They have adroitly traded the limited sculling wobble of the tail for a full-scale shimmy involving the whole body. So lithe and flexible is an eel that if one is caught on a hook, it may tie a simple overhand knot in itself and work its head and the attached fishline back through the knot. Clamping down on the line as it comes through the knot, the eel breaks it or pulls out the hook.

Fishermen and finicky bathers are not the only terrors of an eel's existence. Other fish find small eels to be tasty morsels, and a jarful of pickled elvers is standard equipment in many a tackle box. Only when it is large enough to become the eater rather than the eaten does an eel find the pressure slackening. Even then, the sudden spear of a heron or the razoredged bite of a snapping turtle may cut short the female's seven or eight years in the pond. If she runs the gauntlet successfully, however, she heads back downstream to the coast. Joining the waiting males, she slowly returns to that Sargasso Sea.

Each year a separate migration of eels takes place, and each year a new crop of elvers fights its way upstream past the waterfalls and all its enemies, from fish to fishermen.

The true North American eel is a single species, *Anguilla rostrata*. There are a few other freshwater eels in the world, plus a number of creatures that look like them. One of the most notorious of these ersatz eels is that menace to Great Lakes Fisheries, the sea lamprey.

Actually a lamprey is not an eel at all. It has been

argued that it is not even a fish either. Put simply, it's—well, a lamprey: a circular suction disc armed with rasping teeth beneath the forward end of a long muscular body. The disc and the teeth and the suction can do a terrible job on a lake trout but you need have little worry for your own skin. The ocean lamprey is more a creature of deep water than of bathing beaches. It probably entered the Great Lakes early this century by hitching a ride through canals on the sides of barges and ships.

Peg and I once stood at the Eisenhower Lock on the St. Lawrence Seaway and saw a freighter enter and leave with a couple of two-foot lampreys attached. Short of sending a diver down, however, there was no way to get rid of them. Besides, in this case they were headed out to sea where they belonged.

Luckily, we're learning to cut down the population of the sea lamprey. Such control is cheerful news for jittery bathers—and for all those lake fish, too.

If you're swimming or skindiving in tepid marine waters, you may have qualms about another eel-that-isn't: the moray. Although these creatures have the looks and the ability to live up to their reputations, nearly every moray incident has been traced to some snooping human who pried into the moray's private cave in the corals, or went after it with a spear gun. Both antics, understandably, are resented by the moray.

Although the smaller varieties, about two feet in length, can give little more than a nip and a scare, the six-foot morays can make their point readily with those gaping jaws. So: Hands off!

Actually, you'll probably not meet with a moray, anyway; they are mostly warm-water creatures. So, now that we've brought them up, we can forget them—at least in the north temperate waters covered by this book.

Mention of dangerous fish invariably brings up a discussion of sharks. Here there's some compensation to swimming in the chilly waters of our northeast: many sharks prefer warmer climates. However, there are about a dozen species found from, say, New Jersey north. In fact, a shark perhaps eight feet long surfaced right next to us as we drifted in a sailboat off the Nova Scotia coast. It swam alongside for perhaps half a minute, surveying this tall spindly craft five miles from land. Then, with a swirl, it lazily sank from sight.

Volumes have been written about the pros and cons of sharks as swimming companions. If you plan to indulge in such a pastime, better be well read: there are a number of species that might resent—or overly welcome—your presence. Other species wouldn't hurt you on a bet.

The great basking shark, for instance, feeds only on plankton and similar tiny floating organisms, which it strains from the water to nourish its forty-foot length. On the other hand, a number of sharks less than a third its size may, on occasion, attack anything they can overpower —which, obviously, could include you.

It's a bit difficult to know the species—and the intentions —of a shark when you're swimming around in the water. Even the sharks get confused; during a feeding frenzy among a school of fish, they have been known to attack each other. In such a situation they might make a mistake about *you*, too, if you were available.

Best advice, says the United States Fish and Wildlife Service, is to stay clear of the critters altogether. However, if you're in a shark area, do not swim near anything that may attract them. Fishing on one side of the boat and swimming on the other is taboo: sharks often attack a hooked fish which is spilling blood into the water. If you have any cuts, keep out of the water, too. Sharks are often shy and can be frightened away by splashing, but the smell of blood gives them courage. Fortunately some of the more notorious types, such as the white shark, hammerhead and mako, usually live in deep water and open seas. If you insist on getting in over your head, you'll need more than this book as a life preserver, anyway.

Many "shark" attacks are actually the work of the barracuda. Fortunately, this snag-toothed critter, favorite of fishermen—but not of swimmers—is seldom found north of Florida, although a rare 'cuda has strayed as far as Cape Cod. Best advice about swimming in waters known to be inhabited by barracuda is: don't.

A tiny version of the admittedly dangerous *Sphyraena barracuda* is the harmless little Northern barracuda, *Sphyraena borealis*. It must be a terror among small fish and shiners, but it poses no threat to humans. Living from Cape Cod south, it occasionally shows up in some fisherman's catch, but it's hardly a "baby barracuda." Full-grown, it will barely reach a foot in length.

There are a number of other marine fish and fishlike creatures that may make you wish you'd stayed ashore. Thoughts of stingrays, electric rays and the great manta ray or devilfish have spoiled many an otherwise pleasant day. True, the spine at the base of the stingray's tail can give you a nasty wound, the "torpedo," or electric ray can knock a grown man unconscious, and the manta may exceed ten feet in span and a ton in weight. Chances are that you'll never see a single one of these creatures in the wild, however. And even if you did meet them, they'd have no reason to do you any harm. You scarcely resemble a clam or a pound of fish. You more nearly appear to be some strange enemy. So you and the ray part company—both shaken and glad to be rid of the other.

With those little underwater bulldogs, the sculpins, things may be different. They cannot hurt you, but that's no sign they will not try. One time, while poking around at low tide near some rotted pilings, I felt something striking at my ankle. Looking down, I discovered I was under attack by a pile of pugnacious pebbles. No, it was more like a bunch of souped-up seaweed. That's not a good comparison, either: it was as if a handful of bottom gunk had suddenly been gifted with the power of motion.

While it ineffectually tried to drive my ankle away from its chosen haunts, the sculpin gave me a good look at the improbable way it was put together: head large, pop-eyed, covered with warts and horns, mouth big enough to swallow a hen's egg—but then where would the egg go? The rest of the critter seemed to be an afterthought: all fins and tail and scarcely any body.

Reflecting that the eight-inch little warrior was entirely within its rights in wanting me out of there, I retreated. The sculpin was thoroughly aroused, however. It had me on the run, and wasn't about to quit. It followed me to shore, and even leaped halfway out on land at the finger I waggled at it.

A contentious sculpin could change your attitude toward a wade in the water if it took you unawares. So could the toadfish, a sculpin-like critter with venomous spines—if you're foolhardy enough to thrust an inquiring hand into its rocky cave. And there's a whole ocean of other fish that will scare you out of the water, if you go only by appearances. But, as you size-up some new creature, remember that it is probably doing the same to you. Unless you look like a potential meal—a most unlikely prospect—you'll doubtless be tabbed merely as an unknown.

A momentary curiosity leads your new neighbor to investigate, perhaps, while you steel yourself against such unaccustomed scrutiny. After all, aren't we humans supposed to be the ones to decide whether something is good or bad? Maybe—but nobody has told the fish.

There is a group of creatures bearing the name "fish" that can, indeed, be a hazard to your holiday at the shore. The jellyfish, shaped like umbrellas of various sizes and colors, are relatives of the corals and sea anemones. They are found in all oceans. Perhaps you know them as sea nettles, sea stingers, or sun scalds.

They're well named, too. As they drift through the water, opening and closing every few seconds, these peppery parasols trail many "handles" of long tentacles studded with stinging cells. Size of disc and number of tentacles vary with the species. There are tiny jewels half an inch in diameter and oceanic giants more than seven feet across. One common type (*Aurelia*) is a few inches to a foot wide and a delicate bluish white in color. Its internal organs present a four-leaf-clover appearance. Often you see the "clover" when the rest of the jellyfish is invisible. Its tentacles, around the edge of the disc, are only a couple of inches long, with little power to harm you.

How many jellyfish are there? In point of species, about a dozen common kinds in our northern waters, but in point of total individuals—well, how high can you count? They'll sometimes wash ashore in such numbers that their bodies form windrows on the beach for miles. Swimming

is out of the question at such times. Seaside resorts lose
their customers—except those who weren't planning to
swim, anyway.

Peg and I once sailed with Don and Peg Gill for two
weeks, north of the coast of Maine. Most of the time their
boat plowed through miles of the purplish sun jelly,
Cyanea capillata. The jellies ranged from two inches to
three feet across, with tentacles sometimes twenty feet
long. Anchoring at night, we'd pull up wisps of yellow or
pink tentacles on the anchor chain. Even a fishline would
get tangled with them; touch it carelessly and your hand
would smart for several minutes. Let the line run across
some tender part and you'd carry a burning welt for an
hour.

Jellyfish capture their prey largely by chance. If a tentacle drifts across the body of a fish or swimming crustacean,
hundreds of stinging cells release their little coiled darts.
The darts inject a substance known as hypnotoxin. This
paralyzes the prey, while other cells eject grappling threads
to hang on to it. A slow contraction of the tentacle brings
the hapless fish to the central mouth beneath the disc.

Swimmers have been drowned following paralysis from
contact with these delicate but dangerous creatures. One
of the worst—and most beautiful—is the famous Portu-
guese man-of-war, *Physalia.* It has a pinkish, blue or even
orange gas-filled bladder floating above the surface. The
bladder, ranging up to a foot in length, and shaped like a
cockscomb, catches the wind. It cruises along, dragging a
mass of blue tentacles that may extend as far as fifty feet.
Luckily, the man-of-war does most of its sailing in tropical
seas. I have found a few of its floats on the shores of Long
Island, however; they were probably driven off course by
an unfriendly storm.

It's Going to Sting Me!

Turn a jellyfish upside down, shorten its tentacles, and you have a sea anemone. These plantlike creatures can sting, too, but most of the half dozen species you may encounter in our waters have such a weak punch that you'd never notice it. Small fish, worms and crustaceans, however, are quickly overpowered. They are paralyzed as they come in contact with the many rays of these whitish, brown or purple underwater "flowers."

Some tropical stinging anemones—and jellies such as the man-of-war—have a form of partnership with small fish. Unaffected by the stinging cells, the fish serve as decoys. They go out, excite a larger fish, and lure it into contact with the tentacles. One good jolt, and the tables are turned. The little fish joins its fearsome companion in sharing the scraps of the meal.

The anemones' limy-coated relatives, the corals, are also found in warmer waters than ours. There's little worry about razor-sharp edges and the lethal stings that have done in more than one diver in tropical waters. There's only one coral you are likely to see north of the Chesapeake Bay. This is the small polyp coral, *Astrangia danae*. It forms lumpy little crusts the size of your palm. The crusts are laced with star-shaped pores where the polyps lived. Occasionally you find this coral washed up among seashells on Atlantic beaches.

There is one more group of jellyfish: those known as sea walnuts or comb jellies. Unrelated to the true jellyfish and their cousins—technically known as *Coelenterata*—the sea walnuts do not possess any stinging cells. Instead, these hollow drifters employ rows of paddles to sweep floating organisms into themselves. The paddles bear many movable "teeth," like a comb, and look like the seams of a walnut (hence, "sea walnut"). The combs also give the group its technical name, *Ctenophora*, or "comb bearer."

Comb jellies are dismissed in many biology books as belonging to a minor group of living things. However, if you've ever seen their millions sparkling in the sunny waters of a bay or inlet, you know that at times they can be major, indeed. Ctenophores are completely harmless to us, whether they're the delicate, rainbow-hued sea walnut, the larger (four inches) lovely pink bell-shaped sea slipper, or the six-inch crystal-clear pear jelly.

To sum up the jellyfish story, if you see a cupped or disc-shaped critter that pulsates every few seconds and bears lots of tentacles, watch out. If it's globular, bell-, or pear-shaped without a forest of tentacles, and gliding steadily along through the water, you're safe. Unless, of course, you're some form of little sea creature. Then the cteno-phora will have no more mercy than the coelenterata.

Through the pages of this chapter we've had numerous occasions to congratulate ourselves for the lack of marine monsters in our northern waters. We're in luck when it comes to those characters out of Jules Verne, too: the squid and the octopus.

In truth, the octopus is by nature a shy and inoffensive creature. Its main problem is bad publicity. Our repre-sentative, the retiring Atlantic octopus, is seldom seen near beaches, as it inhabits rocky caves. On rare occasions, it is true, someone accidentally sees one. A child, exploring the rocks in a breakwater from New York City south will come scrambling back with tales of "a giant octopus *this* big" —stretching out both arms.

Actually, half that size would often be closer, with per-haps a couple of feet of spread, arm tip to arm tip. But it'd be hard to prove; the octopus most likely departed the scene faster than the child.

Nearly all "octopus" scares can be traced to that jet-propelled marauder, the squid. Around the northeast such stories would have to be well-nourished by a fertile imagination, however. A jumbo specimen of our largest common squid may reach a length of two feet. Cigar-shaped of body, the squid has ten arms; the octopus eight.

Loligo pealei usually swims by motions of horizontal fins at the end of its body, but it can rocket its way through the water by squirts of a tubular siphon. The only way it could hurt you would be if you were so foolhardy as to pick it up and let it nip you with its parrotlike beak.

Now, the giant squid—that's another matter. Every few years the remains of one of these creatures have been seen along some shore in Newfoundland. Including the outstretched tentacles, *Architeuthis harveyi* apparently reaches the impressive length of fifty feet. And note that word "apparently." Few complete specimens have ever been found.

Doubtless the arm of such a creature, thick as your leg and raised above the ocean, has started many a sea-serpent story on its way. Nor is there reason to doubt that the real thing is much gentler than the myth. A giant squid once attacked a fishing dory off Newfoundland, and it was all the three fishermen could do to escape.

The giant squid is so rare that few museums have a single specimen. So, if one attacks you, rejoice; you're one in a million. And don't let it get away—the museums need it.

Squids and octopuses are molluscs, related to the snail, the oyster and the stodgy clam. I remember reading a story about a shell collector who reached into the water, picked up a killer cone shell, and was fatally stung by the creature's stiletto. Luckily—at least for noncollectors—such venomous molluscs make their home in distant waters.

There are no poisonous shellfish around our beaches. Of course we could get an outsize case of dyspepsia from a polluted oyster or a contaminated clam, but that's our fault, not theirs.

Often lumped in as "shellfish" are those crotchety critters, the crabs and their kin, collectively called the crustaceans. There are about 25,000 species. They range from those pinhead-sized swimming things in swamp water to the crabs and lobsters that, supposedly, like to divide their time between gracing your table and grabbing your toes.

The problem with crabs is that a number of them seem to prefer the same places we do—sandy beaches above and below the water's edge; tidal flats where clamdiggers get in their best work; shallow bays where the fishing's great. Those impish little freshwater relatives of lobsters, the crayfish, lurk under stream banks and shelving rocks. Some of them dig tunnels from the water out into the grass, surmounting the far end of the tunnels with "chimneys" of mud pellets. Reach into a chimney and you may get nipped; pry too closely into the secrets under a mat of waterweed and you'll get the same result. A pinch from the hidden householder suggests that you poke around somewhere else.

One time a small friend, Chris Woelhaf, had a painful experience with a crayfish. A few days later he was peering at a couple of the recalcitrant critters in my aquarium. I decided to try to help crayfish and boy get back into each other's good graces. We watched how the little crustaceans used their long antennae to investigate, how their eyes were on swiveled stalks, and how they used their tails as flippers to scoop backward through the water when danger threatened. I let him drop a piece of liver so it drifted down on top of a crayfish, who immediately turned and seized it. "You see?" I said, giving Chris one last salvo of my ex-biology teacher's artillery, "they can taste food all over their body. They're really quite an animal."

"Yes, Mr. Rood," dutifully agreed my five-year-old friend, "but I still don't like their tweezers."

My young companion's feeling about crayfish spills over onto the sea beaches. Anybody who has ever put a bare foot right into the clutch of a calico crab can agree with him. Also called the lady crab, this common little crustacean has a diameter about the size of a teacup. It's an attractive buff color, with pinkish spots.

The calico crab makes its living in the shifting sands just out beyond wave action—exactly where you like to stand and brave the breakers. As you loom upon the scene, it hastily swims away. If you approach too rapidly, it burrows into the sand, leaving just those stalked eyes exposed. Then, one farther step—and what would *you* do if you were a crab?

The quarter-pound crustacean can not really harm you, of course. Chances are you'll go through several summers before you ever set foot on the few square inches of ocean bottom already occupied by a calico crab. However, when you finally get initiated, the memory will linger on. The rest of that day you'll do a fancy step every time your toe touches a sharp piece of broken shell.

The common spider crab, of the muddy color and the ungainly legs that may stretch two feet from tip to tip, is one of the startling objects you may pull up at the end of your fishline. It is slow and sluggish, however, and aside from the tangle it makes of the line as it tries to tuck the bait into its mouth, the creature is quite inoffensive. You'll probably never stumble into it at a sandy beach, by the way, even if you see its shell cast up by the waves. The spider crab prefers mud and weeds in still or deep water.

The largest of crustaceans is a giant cousin of this non-descript crab. Native to far Pacific waters, the huge oriental spider crab stalks over the ocean bottom like a seaborne basketball player. Scientists, impressed with the spread of the spindly arms, whose total reach may cover twelve feet, tip to tip, have named it *Macrochira*, "big hands." Smaller relatives, a mere half that size, find their way to market as Alaska king crab.

Contrast the lethargic spider crabs with one of the fastest crustacean swimmers: the blue crab, *Callinectes sapidus*. The latter part of its scientific name refers to one of its familiar features: its delicious taste. However, my dictionary says that "sapid" can also mean "agreeable." As far as I've seen, the blue crab is definitely not agreeable; in fact it is—well, decidedly crabby.

It has to be. Crabs seem to be fair game for nearly everything big enough to eat them. In spite of its protective claws, the colorful crustacean with the green body, red-tipped blue legs and white underside faces a constant struggle to keep its armor on its back. That limy covering, unable to stretch, is periodically shed in order that the crab may grow—and appreciative gourmets, human and otherwise, have a meal of soft-shelled crab. A heron, flinty-jawed fish or octopus will make short work of a crab, soft-shelled or not.

The blue crab finds its best defense is in its speed. And thereby lies the margin of safety—both for the crab and for you. With arms that can reach out as much as twelve inches from one claw to the other, Old Crusty could be a formidable opponent. However, it far prefers "the safety of somewhere else," as a fisherman described its ability to escape from danger. Blue crabs dart through the water with all the agility of a fish. Their paddle-shaped last pair of legs scull them sideways so they are little more than a dark shadow.

It is next to impossible to catch a blue crab with a swoosh of a net. You have to ease the net under it while it's feeding on the old fish head you tossed out at the end of a string. Pull the string in s-l-o-w-l-y until the crab is over your net. Then, with an all-out heave, you surprise the crab.

You surprise it, yes. But you may not catch it. It perceives every little motion, and the tensing of your body just as you go into your act may be all the warning it needs. And there you stand, with an empty net and an old fish head.

So, wade right in where the blue crabs are thickest. They'll be ten feet away before you've taken the second step. Since they prefer muddy waters to sandy, two steps may be all you'll wish to take, anyway. But, if by chance, you should capture a blue crab, treat it with respect. Remember, it's a crab. And stay clear of those tweezers.

There's small concern that you'll ever have a showdown with that mitten-handed crustacean, the lobster. Lobsters prefer deep water; how deep, we still do not know. For generations the traditional lobster pot was set, say, in thirty feet of water or more. Now it has been discovered that these one and two pounders are just the little ones. Lobster boats equipped with special gear go as far as fifty miles off our northeastern coasts, staying for a week or more at a time. They return with the great crustaceans ranging from three to thirty pounds. And if you like fish stories, the real big ones may reach three times that weight, according to marine specialists. In truth, nobody knows the size of the world's largest lobster.

What does a king-sized lobster taste like? Peg and I dined on a twenty-two pounder one summer. This one, taken off the coast of New Brunswick, was tougher and less flavorful than much smaller lobsters. However, it was well worth the effort, even if it took a week to demolish it.

One of the most feared—and with least reason—of the hard-shelled inhabitants of the ocean bottom is the horseshoe crab. Shaped like an inverted soup plate with a sawtoothed abdomen and a spiked tail that may be twelve inches long, *Limulus polyphemus* is really not a crab at all. Its closest modern relatives are the spiders and scorpions, but its ancestry is venerable, indeed. Scientists, digging through fossil records, find evidence of this creature's ancestors as far back as 500,000,000 years ago. The horseshoe crab is little changed since that early day.

As strange armored fishes swam in the waters above their heads, the early horseshoe crabs plowed along over the ocean bottom, feeding on ancient clams and worms. Mating in the wave wash of early beaches, they left their eggs in staggering numbers for whatever predators there were to find them—the shorebirds had not yet developed. Neither had the insects, the reptiles, the mammals. Trees were represented by strange plants that looked like logs with hair, or like giant ferns. Only after eons did the dinosaurs appear, flourish and die—while *Limulus* went on, plowing and scattering.

Today, some hundred-plus million years after the last dinosaur, the ancient mariner still makes its springtime pilgrimage to the shallow waters. As we watch the annual invasion of this uncommunicative critter with the tail spike, we can hardly be blamed for our surprise. Try to pick it up and it grips the bottom ocean floor with half a dozen pairs of feet. They pull the shell down into the mud or sand so you cannot reach under the edge. The only thing left to get hold of is that wicked-looking tail. You have to grab fast; the tail, too, is soon buried in the mud.

True, you could impale a foot on that spike. I suppose it has happened, too, but it would have to be on an old shell drifting in the water or cast on the beach. The crab has no intention of bringing its long and successful history to a halt just because you want to go swimming. Like most other water creatures, when it glimpses your scantily clad person approaching, it quickly departs the scene. It can easily skim along the bottom faster than you can walk through the water, so there's little chance that you'll inadvertently catch up to it. Those two compound eyes in the horseshoe crab's "roof," each eye about the size and shape of a small bean in two-foot specimens, may see you only as an ominous dark blur against the sky, but the horseshoe crab seldom stops for a closer look.

Even if you got hold of a horseshoe crab, there'd be little danger. That spike must make an unattractive mouthful for a large fish, but to you it merely provides a handy handle. The pinchers of the largest individuals are little stronger than grasping fingers. So, the next horseshoe crab you see, astonish your friends and pick it up—if you can catch it.

One last spiked denizen of the deep should be mentioned. This one can, indeed, be a problem—but, happily, in our waters it is not a threat. Armed with scores of pointed spines, the peaceful sea urchin is geared entirely for defense rather than offense. Related to the starfish, it shows the same five-sectioned arrangement beneath the spines or on the underside.

As it clings to an algae-encrusted rock or piling, the urchin's wealth of spines makes the globular creature appear as if covered with coarse fur. Scraping with five pointed jaws arranged around a central mouth, the sea urchin feeds on aquatic plant life. When it wishes to sample new pastures, it creeps along on dozens of flexible tube feet, which can inflate or deflate like tiny balloons.

The green sea urchin, *Strongylocentrotus droehbachiensis,* may reach the size of a small orange. Its purple cousin, *Arbacia punctulata,* is about half that size. Although they appear quite prickly, you can pick them up, if you're careful. They are readily harmed by completely fresh water, by the way, so you'll seldom find them above low tide-mark. Those spines would be no protection against a good rainstorm when the tide was out.

The inch-long quills of our little urchins scarcely compare to the lethal-looking needlelike spears of more tropical forms. Some of these are highly irritating and so slender that they break off in the skin. Peg and I, swimming in Hawaiian waters, have floated over rainbow-hued communities of the *wana,* as they are called. They made regular little forests, ten feet below us—red, brown, black, pepper-and-salt, white—their spines of eight inches or more warning us to keep right on swimming.

There are slate-pencil urchins with pinkish-gray clubs like matchsticks, and coat-of-mail urchins with spines reduced to flat plates. Well-nigh invulnerable they are, too, to most enemies. Some creatures, however, have penetrated their defenses. Steely-jawed fish gingerly nip the spines, one at a time, until the urchins are helpless. The formidable crown-of-thorns starfish smothers them with a protrusible stomach and floods them with strong digestive juices. Tiny worms and molluscs creep among the spines and enjoy full protection as they capture other worms and molluscs—or nibble away at their peaceful hosts.

Some seagulls have put gravity to work in helping them. Carefully picking up a sea urchin in its beak, the bird flies high in the air. Dropping the hapless urchin, it allows it to smash on the rocks below. Several tries may be necessary, but each fall breaks off a number of spines until the bird's powerful beak can finish the job. The reward is well worth the effort, too: sea urchins are often crammed with eggs. A favored flat rock or beach of hard-packed sand may be strewn with hundreds of the shells—or "tests"—of urchins—as well as those of unfortunate clams—hoisted aloft and shattered by the gulls.

One gull was apparently outwitted by its own cleverness. Peg and I watched it above the sands of Long Beach, California. It carried its victim to a dizzy height, dropped it, and followed it closely to the ground in accepted seagull fashion. No luck, however, so it repeated the performance —again and again.

We trained our binoculars on the bird, wondering why it was having so much trouble. Then we understood. That seagull was spending its energy on one of the most uncooperative "victims" it could have found: a soggy rubber ball.

It was in those same California waters that I met a real sea monster. It was a calm, sunny day and I was snorkeling among some rocks, peering down at the fantasy of color below me. Peg was snoozing on the shore. For the time there seemed to be just the two of us in the whole world.

Seeing an attractive shell on the bottom, I dived down and secured it. As I started upward, there was a mighty swirl in the water just above my head. Between me and the surface loomed a great shape that seemed to blot out the whole sky.

Shark? Whale? Porpoise? I had no time to think. And,

luckily, I had no time to worry, either. Another swirl, and the Thing revealed itself as a great sea turtle. Suddenly catching sight of me, it gave a mighty heave with those flippers—and vanished off into the sun-dappled depths.

Why had it permitted such a close approach? I could only guess. Perhaps it had come around the corner of a nearby rock while I was on the bottom. Failing to see me, it had drifted, unknowing, on a near-collision course. Or perhaps it had been curious as to this odd being in the water, and had approached for a better look. At any rate, the turtle had had enough. And, for that instant, at least, so had I.

I surfaced, called to Peg, and pointed in the direction it had taken. The turtle, however, stayed below. As far as Peg was concerned, the ocean was as empty as it had ever been. Those great flippers, the light-colored undershell as it swerved away, the bulk that seemed to me as large as a grand piano—but, more probably was no bigger than a card table—they could have all been an optical illusion. Or the product of an active imagination—which is the stuff that most monsters are made of, anyway.

Occasional sea turtles turn up in fishing nets along our northeastern shores, but generally the great reptiles make their living in warmer waters. That unseen river in the sea, the Gulf Stream, flows north a few miles off our eastern coast, however. Doubtless it carries a number of drifters along with it. Occasionally some lost waif strays to a northern beach—and there's another monster.

No, you'll probably never have a heart-stopping visit from a giant turtle in our waters. Not in the ocean, at least. In our lakes and ponds it may be another story. One of nature's most contrary critters is right at home in such places. Friendly as a bear trap, with equal lack of discrimination as to what it bites, the snapping turtle may be found in everything from a farm pond to the Finger Lakes.

The water hazard of a golf course near Burlington was drained one autumn; there, among the golf balls, was a twelve-pound snapper. It was a veritable mossback, with so much algae on its head, feet and carapace that it looked like an oversized divot somebody'd tossed into the water. Our own New Haven River, gurgling clear and often yielding a swift-water trout to a lucky angler, has also provided a home for three of the turtles that I know of—in spite of the crusty critters' preference for much calmer waters.

One reason the snapping turtle gets around so much is that it gets around so much. And that's not double-talk, either: most turtles seem content to remain in a chosen pond, crawling forth annually to lay a clutch of eggs in some nearby sandy bank, and then returning to their old haunts. Old mossback follows the same pattern—except, for some reason known only to her, she sometimes keeps on walking after she has laid the eggs. Here in my mountain town of Lincoln, Vermont, we have found snappers on the hillsides in August—two months and two miles removed from the normal time and place of spring egg laying in the valley ponds.

During such sojourns, the webfooted reptile with the long tail, oversized head and high-legged, dinosaurish gait is out of its native element—and very much on the defensive. Most turtles can pull head and legs into the shell against the attack of an enemy, but not the snapper. Although the upper shell is sturdy enough, the undershell is small and soft. Any turtle is at a disadvantage on its back; the snapping turtle is practically helpless.

The trick, of course, is to turn the snapper over. And

here an enemy runs into violent opposition. That snake-like neck darts out with such a vicious thrust that the creature is sometimes carried off its feet. And once those knife-edge jaws have clamped down, the turtle never lets go.

Well, almost never. *Chelydra serpentina*, "the serpentine water vise," is like a fish out of water when away from its favorite pool. Let it get back home, however, and things are different. Now it is in its element. I have carried a snapper by the tail, carefully holding it away from my legs, while it lunged again and again—at me, at a stick, at everything and nothing. Then, lowering it into the water, I have seen an abrupt change. While I still held it by the tail, the creature immediately tried to swim away, completely ignoring everything in its frantic efforts to escape.

So if by some unfortunate chance you're captured by a snapping turtle, I suppose the best thing to do is head for a tub or a pond, whichever is nearer. And don't worry that you'll already *be* in said pond or tub when the unfortunate event takes place; remember, the snapper's bag of tricks is mainly for self-protection. The rest of the time it is merely intent on getting a meal. All you have to do, therefore, is to keep your toes from looking edible. And, whatever its other shortcomings, the snapper is no fool. If it associates the toes with the rest of you—if, in other words, you splash about in normal human fashion, old mossback will depart for another part of the pond where it's not so crowded. Really.

So, come on in. The water's fine. There's virtually nothing that will harm you. Nearly everything will flee at your approach, or it will just clam up and bide its time until you go away. After all, those waterborne wigglers aren't very fond of sea monsters, either.

Carroll E. Schenk

7·*Eyes in the Evergreens*

"When you're all alone in the dark," my friend Mickey DeCoursey told me, "your imagination works overtime. But this was the real thing. I'd been sitting and fishing on the shore for an hour and my legs got cramped. So I stood up to have a cigarette. When I lit the match I found myself staring right into a pair of eyes."

He rubbed his chin thoughtfully. "Those eyes were on the level with my face and only about eight feet away. The match made a glare, so I held it up over my head to see better. And there I stood, like the Statue of Liberty, when that cussed match went out."

Did he discover what kind of an animal it was? "Well, not right at the moment. When the match burned my fingers I had to drop it. By the time I'd bent over, found my flashlight, and pointed it at the stump where the animal had been sitting, it was gone."

A quick search helped him learn the identity of his silent visitor. The earth near the base of the stump was soft and covered with tracks. There were two types of prints, looking like the impressions left by tiny human hands and feet. The five-fingered "hands," he said, measured about the size of the bowl of a teaspoon, only broader. The hind feet were slender and about an inch longer. They looked like a baby's footprint, complete with an instep and five toes.

His small fishing companion had been that woodland rascal with the insatiable curiosity, the raccoon. Poking along the shore on a fishing trip of its own amidst the gunk and weeds, the ringtail had discovered this curious hulk and had climbed the stump for a better view. When Mickey stood up, the sudden move must have startled the raccoon—but it couldn't resist one last look. Then, at the first opportunity, it fled.

Mickey was startled, too, of course. Nobody would have blamed him if he'd fled, himself, leaving the lakeshore in full charge of the raccoon. However, he was a seasoned woodsman, and doubtless guessed "raccoon" at the first glint of those eyes. These black-masked marauders are quick to scurry up a handy tree at the first sign of trouble.

If you lack the benefit of long experience in the out-doors, however, all those things that glare at you in the dark can be unsettling, indeed. It helps little to remind yourself that there is an equal amount of apprehension on the other end of that flashlight beam. The best thing, per-haps, would be to have an idea beforehand as to what crea-tures you'd logically expect. Then you can coolly run down the list in your mind, select the critter that fits the circum-stances, and with an "aha—wolverine!" you can go about your business.

We'll have more to say about the personalities of these creatures in the next chapter. Right now we're concerned with those portions of their anatomy that catch the beam of your flashlight, the glow of your campfire, or even the flare of your match.

What makes the eyes of an animal shine in the dark, anyway? Do they merely act like a mirror, or do they contain some substance that actually gathers light? The answer is a little of both. The curvature of the eye tends to act as a reflector, just as a dewdrop will glitter in the sun. But this is only part of the story. The tissues of the rear of the eye contain a chemical, guanidine bicarbonate. This compound concentrates the rays of light falling on it —thus, in effect, magnifying even the weakest glow. Most likely this optical property allows the animal to make the most of the dim light of the forest, although the whole process of seeing in the dark is not clearly understood.

Many animals that travel in the dark glitter back at you when you spot them with a light. However, animals of the daytime may do the same. A herd of cows, for instance, often puts on a fine display in the gleam of your headlights as you drive through the country. Cattle seldom travel much after dark, but lie down most of the night. Perhaps their optical system is somehow reminiscing on the days before civilization, when enemies stalked the darkness and they needed the power of night vision.

The eyes of children will reflect a reddish glow for the first few years of life. Many a flash picture shows a blue-eyed father and a brown-eyed mother, say, holding a red-eyed baby. Many of my own early color slides show our four children and their friends enjoying an indoor party or an evening picnic in ruby-eyed glee.

(Incidentally, one way to eliminate such colorful effects is to hold the flash unit a few inches away from "dead center" as you snap the shutter. Thus the reflection is tossed back at the flash instead of right into the camera lens. And, while I'm about it, if you wish to eliminate the glitter of eyeglasses, have your subjects turn their heads slightly away from the camera, thereby bouncing the glitter harmlessly off into space.)

In the animal world, if those gleaming eyes are up in a tree, you've probably got a tree climber—simple as that. But only probably. While you're right to suspect that your arboreal visitor is a raccoon, opossum or flying squirrel (ordinary tree squirrels are usually safely tucked away after dark), it could be something that flew there, rather than climbed—a bird, for instance.

I remember one time when our family was camping in the Great Smoky Mountains. The June night was clear, so we spread our six sleeping bags out under the stars without bothering to set up the tent. Just as we got to sleep the silence was broken by a raucous series of yelps. Apparently our car was parked right on the gravelly spot used by a whippoorwill for his nightly serenades. He'd flown away when we arrived at dusk; now, after things had quieted down, he was back.

We had heard whippoorwills before, but always at a respectable distance. This one was only fifteen feet away. It was so close, indeed, that we could hear the slight "chuck" that precedes each utterance: (chuck) whippoorwill! (chuck) whippoorwill! (chuck) whippoorwill!— nearly once every second, for minutes without stopping.

At first it was fun to lie there and listen to him. The children soon went to sleep, but the din began to get on our nerves. Just about the time we'd get used to the monotony of his rhythm, he'd take a breather. A moment of silence while we nearly dozed off—and it began all over again.

I stood it as long as I could. After all, the bird had his rights. It was his front yard, not ours. But we'd never get to sleep if he kept up that racket. So I got up, took the flashlight, and walked around in front of the car.

He stopped in mid-whip when the light hit him. He crouched for a moment, his pepper-and-salt color blending with the stones and gravel. Then, without a sound, he floated off into the night. Almost instantly his robin-sized body was beyond the beam of my flashlight, but I could follow his progress with no trouble. His eye, the size of a raisin, glowed a fiery red as he circled there in the dark.

I followed him around and around with the flashlight, just like a friend of mine who goes out on Sunday afternoons and exercises flying model airplanes at the end of a long tether. The bird would make a great circle, come in close, then zoom away again—his every move a disembodied spark that blinked out only when he turned away for a moment.

Finally we both tired of the performance. He came to rest on the limb of a large oak a hundred feet away. I climbed back into the sleeping bag. And—you guessed it —just as I was dozing, back he came, as noisy as ever.

More flashlight—this time, I confess, accompanied by a tossed handful of gravel. We both went through the same routine, ending in another stalemate. As I wearily climbed back into the sleeping bag, Peg reached over and handed me a bit of paper tissue. "Earplugs," she said. "They work wonders."

So I fashioned a couple of noise suppressors from two wads of the tissue, covered my head with a crumpled jacket for good measure, and managed to shut that boisterous bird out for the rest of the night. But, even today, when I hear the whippoorwill on the few gravelly roads and ledges where it still returns every spring, it conjures up memories. I can still see that eye zooming through the night like an errant coal from a camp fire.

Those most nocturnal of birds, the owls, bear a magnificent pair of reflectors in the form of those large eyes. Sometimes they glitter so as to nearly blind you when you catch them in the beam of your light; other times they are dark, fathomless pits. I have a picture of the little saw-whet owl that I photographed in the woods behind our house; it shows both the gleam and the darkness of the pupil. Each eye reflects the camera flash as a pinpoint of light, dead center. Outside this tiny luminous speck the pupil is completely black. Then, at the edge of the pupil, the yellow iris shines like a ring of gold. A friend told me that he has taken flash pictures of other owls with much the same result. So, if those eyes up there in the tree seem to have a light-dark-light aspect, center to edge, you may have an owl.

When eyes glare at you from the trees, that's bad enough. When the eyes take to the air and sail right at you, that's even worse. This is just what might happen with a number of the larger insects. The little ones zoom in on your flashlight or camp fire, too, but the glow from their tiny eyes is so weak that you scarcely notice it. Our big moths and beetles, however, can glitter right back at you—and follow the gleam with a personal visit.

The compound eyes of an insect are built of many units, somewhat like the cells of a honeycomb. Capping each unit is a tiny lens, which picks up the light that is directly in front of it. This light bounces back at night just as from a reflectorized highway sign. The insect cannot move its eyes as we can, but the sum total of all those units, arrayed like two halves of a globe over much of its head, allow it to see an almost complete panorama in all directions.

This wide-angle vision is partly responsible for an insect's tendency to make a beeline for you and your light. No matter which way it happens to be turned, it can probably see you—and it takes appropriate action.

Now comes the question: Just why does it fly toward the light, anyway?

The full answer, doubtless, will be forever hidden from us. We are still groping in the field of human behavior; how can you psychoanalyze an insect? But, at least in some cases, there's one thing we *do* know: an insect flies into the light because it cannot help it.

Science has discovered that there's often a close relationship between the light received by an insect's eyes and its ability to fly. As the light enters one eye, the muscles on that side of the body are weakened. The muscles on the other side, being temporarily stronger, turn it toward the weakened (brightened) direction. As it keeps flying, first one side and then the other is affected, and it cannot escape the circle of brightness. Finally, in a tightening spiral, it crashes into the light itself.

Seeing a wayward moth, say, headed toward you on a collision course, you turn off the light. This may bring on a new problem: the sound of that little helicopter buzzing around there in the dark. Give it a minute to regain its night vision, however, and your trouble flies away.

If you're inside a room and find yourself with an unbidden insect guest, darken the room. Turn on an outside light to shine in through the window; the insect will go to the glass. Or open a door into an adjoining illuminated room and the insect obediently departs for the bright lights. Of course what you do then is *your* problem.

Not all insects are attracted by light. Many of those that are active by day—the grasshoppers and butterflies, for instance—pay little attention to all the devices we've concocted to drive the night away. Apparently bright daylight and the complex rays of the sun are needed to stir them to action. The after-dark fliers, on the other hand, react mainly to much dimmer light—until we come along with our lamps and fires and candles and complicate their night life.

Fireflies and glowworms are part of that night life, too. Many of them are fierce little beetles, with an appetite for nearly any insect small enough to catch. In some species, both sexes can fly, while in others only the male has wings. The female, a type of glowworm, crawls around among the grass roots, capturing other insects and sending come-hither messages to prospective mates by means of a gleam of her own.

For all the simplicity of a short flash in the night, the firefly's life is a complex one. If he happens to alight near an already mated female, or if he chooses to land near the female of another species, he may be in danger. She gives him no chance to explain, but may attack him on the spot. Or, for that matter, he may attack her. Obviously such mistakes would be tough for the future of fireflies in general, and one of the unanswered questions is just how he can tell the difference between Glow A ("welcome!") and Glow B ("beat it!"). Does she also make some sinister sound, emit some offensive odor? We just do not know.

Another mystery, which perhaps you have noticed your-self: the great majority of the fireflies in a meadow or field will light up in unison, as if someone were turning a master switch on and off. How do the fireflies over the expanse of an area the size of a football field—about an acre—synchronize so that most of them flash at the same time? Or how, in some tropical fireflies, can the "synch" be so perfect that the whole forest bursts into light, and then suddenly goes dark? We are not sure about that, either.

Nor are we certain as to exactly how the light is formed in the first place. Prying into the luminous organ of a firefly or glowworm, we discover a biochemical pigment, luciferin. It is light-colored, but no more luminous than a lemon peel. Let the firefly release a bit of the enzyme luciferase to act on the luciferin, however, and there's your familiar glow.

Scientists can analyze the reaction and the chemicals involved. They know that the enzyme causes an oxidation of the pigment. But can they repeat it themselves in a test tube? Hardly: the gift of "cold light" escapes us.

Even the eggs may be luminous. It's hard to guess what the use of glowing eggs may be to the firefly, but there they are in some species: eerily biding their time under a leaf or bit of bark. When the larvae hatch out, they, too, bear the luminous trademark. True little glowworms they are, sporting tiny patches like a ship's portholes along the abdomen, or crawling along with an illuminated rear section like the taillight of a tiny car.

Fireflies and glowworms have no option on "cold light," of course. A few other insects can glow. So can some worms in the soil. One time when I was at Scout camp we had a "foxfire fight," tossing pieces of decayed wood permeated with luminous fungi. In my own forest I have found the Deceiving Clitocybe, *Clitocybe illudens*, a mushroom that produces a pale glimmer in the dark.

Peg and I have been swimming at Assateague National Seashore in Virginia when the water was so full of luminous microorganisms that our every motion was outlined in fire. Deeper in the sea are hundreds of glowing fish, squids, jellyfish and worms. Some flash on and off, like neon signs. Others light up only if aroused—when they get a glow on, so to speak. Some are outlined in lights; others display only a spot or two. Such a spot may be a real protection: it gives little hint as to the size and shape of its owner in the darkness of the depths.

Of the land animals, however, there are no common vertebrates in our woods and fields that produce a glow of their own—although one summer, I contemplated the spectacle of an illuminated tree frog. Apparently it had just swallowed a firefly. The unfortunate insect shone out through the translucent innards of the frog for a couple of minutes before its tiny chemical laboratory ran out of oxygen.

I remember reading once about a boy who had become lost in the woods with neither a match nor a flashlight to help cheer his way. As he sat down and tried to compose himself, he realized he was the center of a host of glowing eyes, there in the dark. This, of course, is hardly the way it happens in real life. You'll not be able to count on the shining eyes of animals to help light your way; they will reflect only some beam you toss at them in the first place.

Indeed, your experience with those unknown eyes could be like one I had with a friend on a camping trip in Maine just after graduating from college. Harold Weigold provided the trip as a graduation present, and the two of us headed for the woods north of Poland Spring. We set up our tent and had made a little fire by the edge of a tinkling brook. There was a tiny pool a few yards upstream, and I took flashlight and towel to the pool to wash up for the night.

As I dashed the chill waters in my face and dried with the towel I had the feeling that I was being watched. Reaching for the flashlight, I shone it around through the woodland. Sure enough, the bushes off to my left revealed a pair of eyes. They stared at me steadily, unblinking.

My scalp tingling, I stared back. What was there in the bush? A bear? Wolf? Mountain lion? All kinds of possibilities and impossibilities came to mind, but the eyes gave no clue.

Finally I decided that, since they didn't move, I'd step to one side so I could get a slightly different angle. Perhaps I'd be able to see more clearly. So I moved cautiously to my right and discovered a surprising thing: only one eye glowed. The creature was apparently staring straight ahead, and not at me at all. Heartened by this revelation, I cautiously moved nearer.

At last I was close enough to pick out the mysterious animal's shape and color. There it was, cradled beneath the bush and doing precisely what its forebears had done for centuries.

Keeping perfectly still and not varying so much as a hair, no matter how I moved about, was my threatening woodland adversary: a dappled, newborn fawn.

8 · Menacing Maneaters

"Yep," the game warden said, "it sure is funny. Every case I've ever heard about a she-bear with cubs attacking somebody, that somebody always had a gun."

We were sitting in his office in Montpelier, chatting about the wild mammals that roam our northeastern countryside. We'd been through coyotes and wildcats, weasels and mink. We speculated on whether there were wolverines in Vermont ("I've never seen one, Ron, but they're north of us in Quebec. And wolverines don't give a hoot about international boundaries"). Finally our talk got around to bears.

"Guess I'd better qualify that statement about she-bears," he added. "I'm speaking about our eastern black bear. I don't claim to know much about other bears—grizzlies and such. And I wouldn't give much for your chances if you *did* get between a black bear and her cubs. The thing is, it just ain't going to happen."

Her senses of smell and hearing, he pointed out, "are so keen that the old she-bear knows you're there almost before you know it yourself. And when you've got no gun —when you have to go your way and she can go hers— everything ends up real peaceful."

And he ought to know. Vermont, the last time I checked, has about one black bear for every two square miles on the Green Mountain National Forest. This is about as dense a bear population as any national forest in America. Over the thirty-plus years of his experience as a warden, he's seen his share of bears, too. "And not once, Ron, have I known a healthy, unwounded black bear to do anything but clear out of there after you arrive."

In spite of such heartening words, people continue to wonder about what would happen if they met Old Bruin around the next bend in the path. Indeed, Peg's father once had such an experience in his early years as a forester. Hiking down an overgrown logging road, he happened upon a bear absorbed in tearing a log apart for ants and grubs. Suddenly realizing it had a visitor, the animal stood up on its hind legs, not twenty yards from his awestruck gaze.

"It looked about ten feet tall," Don Bruce told me. "And I was scared enough to drop in my tracks. But the way it was sniffing and squinting at me, I figured it didn't really know who or what I was. I couldn't move, anyway, so I just stood there."

There was no question as to when the bear finally got the scent. "It jumped as if it'd been hit," he said. "Then it turned and crashed off through the bushes—going 'wuff, wuff, wuff!' all the way."

Surprised like that, even the inoffensive black bear could be a dangerous customer. Better to arrange things so the unexpected doesn't occur. If you're in bear country, sing or talk when you're in densely wooded cover. You may not see many birds or wildlife, but you'll not see any bears, either. Your noisy, smelly, brush-crackling presence persuades *Ursus americanus* to make himself scarce

Most of the semitame bears in our national parks are black bears, too—even the brown-furred ones. The lighter "cinnamon" shade is merely a color phase. Sometimes a mother will have one cinnamon cub and one black cub in the same litter.

There is far more to be cautious about in connection with these bears—whatever their color—than with the truly wild ones away from the picnic areas. In spite of repeated warnings, people feed them and try to pet them. Peg and I still shudder at the thought of a six-year-old girl we saw at Algonquin Provincial Park, north of Toronto. The girl was feeding fig bars one by one to a bear while her doting parents urged her on so they could take her picture with a movie camera. Luckily, the bear was content to receive its cookies one at a time instead of grabbing for the box she held just out of its reach—or those foolhardy parents would have gotten some fancy home movies, indeed.

The worst example of such stupidity was told us by a ranger at Great Smoky National Park. "A bear had stopped a car, begging for a handout," he said. "The man had climbed out of the car with his camera, leaving the door open. His wife stayed inside with a bag of sandwiches. When I got there, the wife was coaxing the animal into the car with the sandwiches, while the man pushed on its rear end. That idiot was trying to get the bear behind the steering wheel so he could take a picture of it 'driving' the car."

The ranger shook his head in disgust. "And the thing that's worse: If the bear had attacked either of them, I'd have had to shoot it. Yet you know who really should've been shot. It was a pity that all I could do was arrest the both of them."

If you're in a campground that may be visited by bears, be sure you leave no tidbits out where they may tempt the great creatures. Hang fragrant items such as bacon in a tree if you must, but remember that black bears can climb. Better to wrap the bacon in airtight plastic or put it in a container with a close-fitting cover. As added precaution, store it a safe distance away from where you plan to sleep.

I recall one night when Peg and I were tenting with our four kids at Yellowstone National Park. We carefully put the food away in the car, unrolled our sleeping bags on the tent floor, and lay there watching the bears on their visits to the garbage cans. We could hear a bottle tinkle or a can rattle as they rummaged for tidbits. Now and then a dark hulk would shuffle past the doorway, but as none of us had so much as a chewing gum wrapper in the tent, the bears paid no attention to us.

Just as I was getting drowsy, a vehicle drove up to the adjoining campsite. I could hear its occupants moving about for a few minutes. Then I dropped off to sleep.

When we arose we discovered that our neighbors were a man, woman and girl in a pickup-truck camper. Nodding good morning to them, I noticed that they were about to drive away.

"Well, you sure didn't stay long," I said, making conversation.

"No, *sir*," said the man. "Not with those bears!"

In answer to my puzzled look, they told their story. Arriving late and hungry, they had tossed a steak onto the tiny stove in the camper. Then, dog-tired, they had stacked the dirty dishes, pulled down the covers, and piled into bed.

No sooner had they settled down, however, than there was a splintering of glass. A great paw reached through one of the louvered side windows. It groped around for a moment, disappeared, and then returned. At the same time they could hear the labored breathing of a bear as it tried to hoist itself up to where it could climb in the window.

There was the sound of toenails scratching on the camper's fragile aluminum shell. They heard the frustrated whine of the animal as it sought to get at the source of that delicious steak aroma. After a moment the bear dropped to the ground and began sniffing along the lower edge of the camper body. Then it began pulling at the door.

Horrified, they leaped out of bed. The mother and daughter grabbed the door handle while the father ransacked the sink for the butcher knife. In his desperation, there in the dark, he knocked over the pile of dishes.

That clumsy move was a lifesaver. The din of clattering pots and pans was enough to startle the bear. It dropped down on all fours and scurried away. Pausing after a short distance, it contemplated the camper. Then, as the family collapsed with relief, it ambled off into the night.

Hastily they washed the dishes and threw their bag of scraps out toward the garbage can. Then, still shaking, they tried to salvage a few hours' sleep. Every sound wakened them, however, so they passed the rest of the night in misery.

And all of this took place while we slumbered in safety

in our flimsy tent only twenty yards away!

The point, of course, is that, as with almost any wild animal, your problem comes when you interfere with its normal way of life. And plunking a sirloin steak right on a bear's doorstep hardly qualifies as noninterference. A completely wild bear would smell the steak just as well, but the overpowering presence of people would warn it to keep its distance. With a campground animal, however, the warning has been dulled by long association with humans. And if familiarity breeds contempt, several hundred pounds of overgrown teddy bear can be quite an armful of familiarity.

Personally, I've had more problems with the bear's diminutive cousin, the raccoon. I've been bitten twice—both times my own fault—because of this familiarity-contempt syndrome. Although the sheer bulk of a bear inspires caution, what can be so bad about a frisky, inquisitive, ten-pound, four-legged coonskin cap?

So you overstep the bounds of caution and plant a playful pat on that furry derriere as Ringtail reaches headfirst down into a garbage pail. Then you discover something, and quick: beneath that easygoing exterior lurks a spitfire.

That's just how I contracted my first raccoon bite, by the way. Little *Procyon lotor* had forced the lid off a trash can and was rummaging through the contents. I contemplated the only portion of him that was visible: a broad rear porch that wobbled about as he tugged at some uncooperative tidbit. He seemed so absorbed in what he was doing that I sneaked up to touch him.

How he heard me coming, I do not know; but as I reached out, the raccoon changed ends. Just like that.

Where there had been a peaceful ball of fur, there was now a snarl and a double row of white teeth. Even as I recoiled, the animal sprang forward. It caught the skin of my hand, gave a wrench, and dropped to the ground. Almost before I realized I'd been bitten, the raccoon bounded off into the dusk.

Those memorable few seconds transpired during my college years at the University of Connecticut. The recollection of them stayed with me for a couple of decades. One day a friend asked me to help extricate a raccoon that had blundered through the eaves and into the attic of an old farmhouse. It had been there for several days and couldn't find its way out.

Remembering how raccoons can bite, I donned a heavy jacket and gloves on that July day. Carrying a wadded-up army blanket for a weapon, I advanced into battle.

The blanket, of course, was to throw over the animal so I could bundle it downstairs and out into freedom. But the attic was hardly spacious enough for such maneuvers. Besides, the sweat was already running down into my eyes so that sometimes I saw two raccoons—or none at all. When I made my move, pouncing on that black-masked bandit, the bandit scooted right past me.

When I located that critter again in the dim light, it was at the other end of the attic. Once more the advance and attack; once more the escape. Then, back on hands and knees the length of the attic to do it again.

By this time, I was drenched with sweat and getting madder by the minute. Why'd I ever let the guy talk me into this, anyway? *Now*, you cussed Ranger Rick—pounce —I'll getcha!

I got him, too. Got him by the ankle—my ankle. Know-

ing exactly where he'd go on his next dash, I kicked
him as he went by. The gleam of bare skin between shoe
top and pants' cuff gave him a bull's-eye to retaliate. He
tried for a mouthful, and got a fair substitute. But that
little pause slowed him just enough. Whirling like a raccoon myself, I crashed down on him—blanket and all.

Scooping the animal up, I clutched his struggling form
to my bosom. Descending the ladder to the welcome cool
of the bedroom below, I presented myself, all sweat and
gore, in front of my friend.

My former friend. He was sitting on the bed, calmly
smoking a cigarette.

"Here!" I exploded. "Here's your stupid raccoon!"

Infuriated at people who send you up into hot attics to
get bitten by raccoons—and doubly mad at myself, the supposed expert on animals, for such a botched-up job—I
stalked out of the house. He followed close behind, utter-
ing words of great comfort while I silently hoped my ankle
was leaving an accusing trail of blood with every step.

Outside, I dumped the raccoon on the lawn. The poor
creature landed at full gallop and vanished forever into
the weeds.

I've had several similar performances over the years.
They have, indeed, made me an expert—an expert, that is,
on how not to underestimate any living creature. And such
hard-won wisdom brings me back to the point of this chapter: every nerve and fiber of a wild animal's body is tuned
to its own struggle for existence. There is little room in its
life for dalliance with nonessentials like you and me.

Take, for instance, one of the frequent questions that
may spring up around the camp fire. A twig snaps, out
there in the dark, or your little dog suddenly growls and

gets to his feet, hackles raised. Only an opossum, you decide, or a flying squirrel. But what if it's something else? What are your chances, for instance, of meeting a wolf?

Surprisingly, the chances are getting better—or worse, depending on your viewpoint about wolves. Not the great timber wolf, *Canis lupus*, that vanishing monarch of the wilderness, but a wolf just the same: *Canis latrans*, the coyote or prairie wolf. You may meet the coyote on farm- or brushland almost anywhere in the western two-thirds of North America. It is still doing quite well, even in some areas where it's been hit with everything from arsenic to airplanes. It's a resourceful critter, getting along on its wits, and is even extending its range in some areas.

Perhaps its slowly expanding range is responsible for some new "wolves" that have appeared east of Buffalo. They were reported back in the 1940's and even earlier, but few people paid much attention to scattered tales about them. Now they have been sighted over most of our northeastern states and adjacent Canada.

In appearance, these creatures average somewhat larger than the coyote. One female that I examined weighed thirty-five pounds—perhaps ten pounds heavier than an average female coyote. Shaggier, often rangier in appearance, these "coy dogs," as they've been called, were long assumed to have descended from a cross between a farmer's dog and a traveling coyote. They were seen in the woods, along the fence lines, even right out in the open.

Many scientists now feel that the animals are not half-breed dogs at all, but some new, twentieth-century wolf. Perhaps they are a subspecies of the true coyote; perhaps some kind of an offshoot of the timber wolf. Whatever they are, their numbers seem to be increasing. My own state of Vermont is estimated to have at least two thousand, although they move around so much and vanish so quietly that an accurate count is impossible.

There are several of these bigger-and-better coyotes within a mile of our house as I type these words—unless they are twenty miles away. Like most members of the dog family, they are tireless travelers, and we may be sharing our little pack of "coy dogs" with someone halfway to Burlington. I can occasionally hear their yipyip-yo-o-o-o in the woods; it's less musical than the serenade of the true coyotes, and quite different from the barking of a dog, but it's thrilling to hear on a wintry night. Our friends, Dan and Diane Adam, a mile away through the woods, have seen five of them in an abandoned pasture.

This, of course, brings up a question. Coy dogs, coyotes, whatever they are—how will they act if you meet them in the wild?

First, notice that word "if." Remember, those super senses are supposed to keep them away from trouble—and trouble, in this case, could mean *you*. The most you can expect to see is a swiftly running brown animal with a straight, low-slung tail, disappearing through the brush.

On a rare occasion, however, should you surprise a coyote, western or eastern, you may be in for a treat. Gifted with an outsize curiosity along with its other attributes, the coyote may be reluctant to flee. In checking you out further, it can put on quite a performance.

A friend of mine, Buddy Lafayette, was fishing a woodland stream. Slowly wading along, considering the possibilities of the next pool, he looked up and saw three coyotes sitting on the bank and watching him. When they realized they had been discovered, they barked and ran. Circling, they came back and barked again. .

"First they were on one side of the brook, and then on the other," he said. "They'd keep barking and looking and jumping. They made such a ruckus that the fishing was no good, anyway. So I cleared out of there."

Were they working up their nerve for an attack? "Oh, no," said this young man, who has practically grown up in the woods. "Not at all. You can tell the difference in an animal's attitude. They were put out because I was there. Chances are they'd never seen anybody standing quietly in the middle of the stream before. They probably couldn't get over it."

I have not had any such opportunity to see *Canis whatsis* put on this kind of a show, but I recognized Buddy's description of that behavior. Such hijinks are common in the dog family. Don Brown, another friend, told of a similar performance by a red fox.

The fox had been poking along a stone wall when Don happened to drive past. Stopping, he reached for his camera to take a picture "and that fox jumped up and down, stiff-legged, yapping and whining. It turned a tiny circle, as if chasing its tail, and even made a couple of dashes at the car. Carried on for about five minutes—best act you ever saw!"

As it turned out, the fox's antics were a canine version of the broken-wing act put on by a number of mother birds when their young are in danger. Don Brown, although absorbed with his camera, suddenly wondered just why the performance was taking place. Glancing up at the right time, he saw the elfin faces of a couple of cubs peeking over the wall. The mother was putting on such a display that they couldn't resist looking, too.

Buddy Lafayette's experience may also have indicated there were young cubs nearby. Coyotes have strong family ties, and the three that he saw might have been a parent and a couple of adolescents protecting a litter of youngsters.

At any rate, if you're privileged enough to witness such a performance, there's little reason to figure your days are numbered. Even with the great timber wolf, which sometimes travels in packs of two dozen, there has never been a proven case of an unwounded animal willfully attacking a human being—in spite of the comment by some wag that no human being would live to report such an onslaught, anyway.

There are still a few isolated spots where you'll stand a slim chance of seeing the real timber wolves, by the way. At Algonquin Provincial Park in Ontario, the wolves still roam the forests. In summer the rangers lead the campers on periodic "wolf howls." Gathering in the dark, as many as a thousand persons listen as a couple of rangers raise their voices in an inviting wail.

Often their efforts are met only by silence. Occasionally, however, there is a thrilling answer: a distant howl—long, low and primeval. Even more rarely the call triggers a chorus that echoes across the valleys in one of the grandest symphonies of nature.

There are timber wolves in other parts of Canada, as well. The United States can claim a few in Michigan, Minnesota and other border states, as well as Alaska. One spring I traveled with Stephen Greene, who has published several of my books, to Isle Royale National Park in upper Lake Superior. Isle Royale contains more than a hundred square miles of woods, brush and streams. It is almost uninhabited except for a few summer vacationers.

There are about two dozen wolves on the island. They

are so adroit at keeping hidden, however, that most camp-ers have no inkling they're around. Steve and I were there before the camping season, but although there was fresh evidence of the great creatures about the campground each morning, we neither saw nor heard a single wolf.

We traveled with three biologists, Mike Kochert, Larry Roop and Dr. Michael Wolfe, to inspect the remains of a couple of moose that had been killed by the wolves. Both carcasses were those of aged females, one nearly toothless and crippled with arthritis, while the other was handi-capped from an old hip injury. The wolves, opportunists that they are, had really done those suffering moose a favor.

Along the woodland trails we observed wolf "scats," or droppings, and witnessed where they'd turn aside, here and there, to water a favored stump. But never so much as a single howl or a sudden distant movement met our ears or eyes. "But don't feel too disappointed," said Mike Wolfe. "I studied them myself here for three years before I met one face to face on the trail."

So you're in little danger from wolves, whether big, little, or modern middle-sized. Red Riding Hood, the Three Pigs, and Peter and the Wolf make fine stories—but only stories.

The same is true of foxes, by the way. Aesop's foxes catch crows and geese but, even in the fables, they never molest people. Don Brown and the performing fox were fascinated with each other, but neither meant any harm. I've had foxes bark at me, too, and even had one follow me about two hundred feet back along a woodland trail like a little dog. Curiosity—that's all.

A friend of mine told about a red fox that lingered at the edge of a woodland clearing where he was sitting one autumn afternoon. As my friend made no threatening move, the fox gained enough courage to approach within about fifty feet. The man slowly reached down, grasped a stick, and tossed it toward the animal. "And, bigosh, that fox picked it up and tossed it in the air and played with it just like a dog. When he ran off into the woods he was still carrying it."

A full-grown fox is about as big as an outsized tomcat. Thus it's hardly in a position to harm you, even if it would. In the cat family itself, there are critters gifted with a generous helping of curiosity, just as in the wolves and foxes. Frank Hier, an avid hunter and fisherman, has had a wildcat accompany him along the trail, just a few paces back, first on one side and then on the other. Such behavior on the part of a wildcat—or bobcat, if you prefer—could be decidedly upsetting if you didn't realize it had no sinister motive.

In a way, that wildcat was only being human. Consider for a moment: we train our binoculars on birds and animals; we photograph them; we read books about them. Our consuming interest drives us to snoop into their birth, their death—even their sex lives. We weigh them, measure them, hang their heads over our fireplaces, even adorn them with radio transmitters so they don't have any secrets left. Yet if an animal does a turnabout; if it has enough interest in us not to flee at our approach—heavens! Will it bite me?

Here in Vermont the stories continue about the legendary Vermont panther. Every few months someone sees it. Known variously as painter, cougar, mountain lion, puma or catamount, *Felis concolor* ("the cat that's all one color") was once native to most of North America, coast to coast.

Now largely confined to southern swamps and western hills, it could, indeed, make its way back into a bit of its former range on occasion. To paraphrase Thor Heyerdahl, who was asked if a certain strange creature might have approached his raft *Kon Tiki* on its voyage, "just because I haven't seen it doesn't mean it's not there."

Perhaps that's the way with the panther. One of the least bold of cats, it shuns the presence of man. At 150 pounds or more, and six feet to the tip of its tail, it could give a good account of itself, but it would rather flee than fight. Melting away into the forest, it may, indeed, still be there.

Once the panther could retreat to the back country, but now that country has people. My game warden friend in Montpelier feels it'll be just a matter of time before someone photographs a northeastern panther "or until some fool shoots one because it's the only one he's ever seen."

So, with regard to a mountain lion on your vacation in the mountains, my suggestion would be the same as his: take along your camera. It's a long shot, but you may be the one to get that first photograph.

Quite often the purported "panther" is a black animal. This may be another creature of our northeastern woodlands: the "fisher cat" or fisher. Like the catamount, it has a long, impressive tail. It's very much at home in the trees, too; despite its three-foot length, it can catch a squirrel.

The fisher is actually a member of the weasel family. It is long and lithe, as are its smaller cousins, the weasel, the mink and the ferret. It can give a murderous account of itself in a battle, but it is so retiring that it will seldom stand and fight.

Confined to the northern woods, the fisher is most at

home in Canadian forests, plus those in upstate New York and northern New England. Even there you'll be lucky if you ever see it. Preferring solitude, it could conceivably peer at you from the banks of the Allagash in Northern Maine. But at Call-O'-the-Wild Campground with trailer hookups? Never.

A bit longer and much heavier than the fisher—up to forty pounds, compared to the fisher's eighteen—the wolverine is the largest North American member of the weasel family. It's thicker set than most of the other weasels, with sturdy legs and a powerful body. Dark, with a grizzled gray stripe along its side, the wolverine has been described as looking like "an undersized bear with an oversized tail."

There's nothing undersized about its reputation, however. For centuries the wolverine has commanded its share of vituperation from trappers, lumbermen, and early French *voyageurs*. A confirmed opportunist, with the strength and ability to take advantage of most any situation, the wolverine will follow a trap line through the woods, taking trapped animals, upsetting traps and spraying the area with urine or with the fetid musk from glands near the base of its tail. No wonder the French-Canadians call it *loup garou*—the werewolf!

Traveling through the back country at a tireless lope, the wolverine may happen along just as a bear is engaged in a meal. Putting on a display of ferocity that overwhelms the peaceful bruin, it appropriates the feast for itself. Or, sniffing out the hidden food cache of a north woods trapper or camper it takes what it can eat, then helpfully sprinkles the rest with a musky "don't touch: this is mine."

Even biologists are impressed with the capacity of the glutton, as it is sometimes called. Needing an appropriate epithet, they came up with just the right scientific name:

Gulo gulo (though it is also classified as *Gulo luscus*) "the throat with a throat."

Yes, if you're a delicious half-grown raven in a treetop nest or a northern beaver that has strayed too far from the protection of the pond, you have much to fear from the wolverine. But if you're a human being? You've read this so often in these pages now that you can say it with me: "if you do not bother it, it will not bother you."

There's another reason you'll not have to worry about a wolverine. Caring little for man and his machines, it keeps well to itself. Retiring farther into the vastness of the north woods at the first sound of a transistor radio, it is seldom seen, seldom captured: a living legend that has accomplished the most prodigious feats ever perpetrated by a living creature. And if it didn't actually do them, it could have.

Little cousin of the wolverine, and just as mighty in its own way, is the common skunk. Almost everybody knows the reputation of our eastern skunk, *Mephitis mephitis* ("poison gas"—what else?) and the striped creature has been reported right within the confines of New York City. It's a member of the weasel family, bearing the musk glands common to most weasels, but without the typical weasel temperament. The skunk lives according to a philosophy of a just and lasting peace. Unlike many pacifists, however, it carries the authority to back up its desires.

You could, indeed, come to grief in an encounter with a skunk. Easygoing and even-tempered as it may be, its small size still gets it in trouble. Dogs are tempted to attack this plume-tailed wood kitty, and cars are forever running over it as it putters along the roadside looking for travel trash. Then, too, you may walk into your garage some night and suddenly discover that the garage is already occupied.

And not only the garage. Also, in a few minutes, the entire vicinity: front yard, backyard, neighbor's yard and your whole house. Your sudden appearance doubtless brought forth a preliminary tail-hoist from old *Mephitis*, but, dark as it was, you failed to notice. Whistling or humming or just groping for the light switch, you waded right ahead. Perhaps there was a stamping of those little front feet, too—a warning you should have heeded. And then. . . .

Skunks can shoot from any angle; it's not true that they have to get into a certain position to fire. However, since accuracy is important in the presence of a determined enemy, the skunk often forms its body into the letter "U" —head and tail both facing the foe. Thus it can see what it's doing. It can vary the spray from a fine mist to a tiny jet that may squirt as far as ten feet.

Don't be misled into believing that a skunk cannot spray if you lift it by the tail. True, sometimes the unusual position will render the anal glands incapable for the moment, but once you've got the skunk, how are you going to let go?

If you *do* find that you've been occupying Ground Zero, and the skunk has scored a perfect bull's-eye—or an equally devastating near miss—you'll be interested to know what to do next. Should the spray get in your eyes, it will cause great pain and temporary blindness; wash the eyes with copious quantities of water. If the gas attack also included your dog or cat, the traditional sponge bath with tomato juice gives fairly good results. Best treatment for your own clothes is to hang them out in the sun and air. The oily spray is volatile and will succumb to the effect of a few days of warm, dry sunlight.

One precaution, however: don't wear those clothes on damp days. The smell may return, slightly, and you may find you've come out last in a popularity contest.

Mention skunks as possible perils and someone will also bring up the subject of porcupines. Peg and I have had a number of experiences with porkies; we've even had a couple as star boarders in our household for more than a year apiece. The only way you'll ever get stuck by a porcupine—and here's the same old story again—is if you molest it.

Erethizon dorsatum ("the irritable back") is at peace with the world, just as is the skunk. While the skunk spends most days sleeping off the results of the previous night's foray after grubs, mice and frogs, the quill-pig may be active day or night.

Well, not exactly active, but at least it may be visible— up in a tree, perhaps, where it contentedly gnaws the twigs, buds and bark. At other times it waddles through the woods, nibbling at local greenery—plus such delicacies as axe-handles, doorknobs or other objects that may have the salt of perspiration on them.

So great is the porky's fondness for salt that my Vermont neighbors sometimes pour salt on an old unwanted stump—and allow the porcupines to nibble it to the ground. The placid rodents may also gnaw automobile tires after a car has been run on winter roads that have been strewn with salt to melt the snow. The resulting explosion may scare the wits out of the porky, but the owner of the car usually fails to see the humor of the situation. Surveying as many as four flat tires after he has left his car parked in a good porcupine woods, he takes to the warpath with blood in his eye.

This brings us to the point, so to speak: those murderous quills. It is true that an enraged porcupine, quills raised on back and tail, may whirl around and strike some object, thus causing a loose quill to fly through the air. The quill, however, is really just a modified hair and the porky has no power whatsoever to "throw" it even a fraction of an inch. Of course, those incredibly sharp, barbed black points are all but invisible, and may cling to an enemy at the slightest touch, so it appears that the animal *did* throw the quills, even if it didn't really happen.

Suppose you do get close enough to collect a few quills, or your dog gets a snootful in a rash moment, what's your next course of action?

Well, there are various remedies. Many suggestions get at the hollowness and stiffness of these slender stickers. "Soak them in vinegar," one person says. "Lemon juice is better," says another. Warm milk is suggested, along with warm water, mineral oil or castor oil—all applied to the offending quills and adjacent skin.

A friend of mine in Starksboro has his own remedy. "Plenty of whiskey'll do it every time," he states. "Outside and inside. Softens the quills and makes you real happy, too."

There are also those who suggest that the outer end of each quill be snipped off to allow the air to escape from its hollow structure. However, there is little or no air in that slender tip. Besides, one problem with a struggling dog is just to get close enough to touch it in the first place —to say nothing of snipping away with scissors.

The best course, in most cases, is the most direct one: pull them out with pliers. Those sharp points are armed with backward-pointing barbs, so they tend to work deeper into the flesh with every motion. Thus, time is essential. If there are just a few quills, you may be able to enlist the aid of a friend as you de-sticker your pet. If your pup got a good dose—and I've seen dogs with so many quills that they looked as if they'd grown a grizzled, two-inch beard —better to bundle your crestfallen companion off to the veterinarian.

You may find the placid porky almost anywhere in our northeastern woodlands—especially from the latitude of southern Massachusetts up into Canada. You may find it any time of the year, too, in all but the fiercest winter blizzards. My friend Bob Douglas, who has an orchard next to a woodland, saw a porcupine that stayed in an old apple tree for nearly a month. It was there, night and day, through every kind of weather—and if you're familiar with Vermont in late winter, you know that such endurance is a noble feat, indeed.

Most of the time, whether you're in a porcupine paradise, the bailiwick of a bear or even the precinct of a puma, you'll probably have nothing to worry about. It's true that people have been chased out of the woods by a buck deer in mating season, and more than one hunter has been treed by a bull moose in rut. Such performances are rare, however; in fact, so rare that they become front page news when (and if!) they ever happen.

Most of the time you're just as safe among these menacing maneaters as you are in your own home. In fact, safer, when you consider slippery bathtubs, loose stair treads— and the automobile that took you out into the woods in the first place.

Indeed, even if you hike to that hideout you may be in dire peril. A step or two may be all it takes. Peg drove her car to kindergarten one chilly day, deposited it carefully in the parking lot, stepped out onto the only patch of ice in the whole town of Middlebury—and spent the next four months on crutches because of a broken leg.

CALAMINE
LOTION

9·Perilous Plant Life

Time was when you could walk down a country lane or a suburban street in spring or fall, sniffing appreciatively at the aroma of burning leaves. Occasionally a wisp of smoke caressed you as you passed by. You nodded a cheery hello to the man with the rake who'd provided the smoke—and then you went home to nurse a beautiful case of poison ivy.

Those days are gone. At least they're gone in areas where do-it-yourself home landscapers obey the law. "No open burning" is now the decree over much of our continent. Thus those pungent reminders of the passing of the seasons have gone the way of the top-down convertible from which it was so pleasant to take everything in—including a whole countryside's worth of burning poison ivy in an afternoon.

Yes, it's true: you can, indeed, get poison ivy from the smoke as it burns. Tiny droplets of the irritant resin in tissues of the plant may cling to particles of ash and soot that settle down on you.

That's getting poison ivy the unorthodox way. You can get a more respectable dose if you yank it up by the roots, even after the leaves have fallen and it looks dry and harmless. Or—as happened on one memorable occasion to a city cousin who'd never been exposed to anything more dangerous than muggers and taxicabs—you can carefully select a bouquet of the glossy foliage for a centerpiece.

The traditional way to meet poison ivy, however, is just to blunder into it. Growing as it does along roadsides, lakeshores and waste areas, the plant may be lying in wait as you decide to pause and relax on a backpacking trip, say, or as you spread a ground-level picnic in the summer sun. Then, too, hikers and campers, off alone in the bushes, may make a highly personal acquaintance with it as they're out doing what hikers and campers do when they're off alone in the bushes.

Poison ivy can be a real hazard in your outdoor travels. You may run into it—literally—almost anywhere from Maine to California and up into Canada, excluding deserts, swamps and deepest forests. Scrub oaks and pines of the southeast are usually free of poison ivy, too, as may be oak and hickory woodlands farther north. But since a good dose of it may put you in the hospital, it's better to know the pesky plant for sure than to go somewhere and hope it won't bother you because it's not supposed to live there. Besides, some of those scrub oak and pine areas are fine habitat for poison oak, so you may still get nailed.

After you become familiar with poison ivy you can spot it in a number of ways—its habit of climbing up the trunks of large trees, for instance, or its manner of enclosing a stone wall in a solid mass of green. In the winter its trailing vines with their erect branches may bear clusters of whitish-yellow berries, and in the spring its tiny new leaves show glossy red sprinkled with green.

It's the leaves themselves that give the best clue to the identity of poison ivy. Usually (but not always) shiny on the upper surface, each leaf is made of three pointed leaflets on little individual stems, sort of like an expanded clover. Sometimes the leaflets are notched or lobed, sometimes smooth along the margin. There are often little "radicals" —rootlike structures by which the ivy clings to a ledge or treetrunk. Thus the scientific name becomes a perfect description: *Toxicodendron radicans*, "the poisonous plant with little roots."

The ivy's first cousin, poison oak, is *Toxicodendron quercifolium*, referring to the resemblance of the leaves to those of some of the oaks, *Quercus*. In parts of this country, the term "poison oak" actually describes poison ivy, both being so closely related in the sumac family. Otherwise the two plants can be treated the same: with great respect.

There are other three-leaflet plants, by the way: strawberry and raspberry, for instance, and some roses. The shine on the ivy leaves should be a help in identification. Poison ivy also bears small greenish-yellow flowers that can hardly compare with the attractive white berry blossoms or the bloom of the rose.

Once you've identified those leaves, don't make the mistake that Peg did when she was a girl. She had heard the familiar story that if you munch on a bit of poison ivy you'll become immune to it. No such luck. Peg tried it and ended up with fiery, itching blisters inside her mouth and throat. She missed a session of Girl Scout camp, could barely swallow, and spent a couple of weeks in bed.

Nowadays there are preventive injections that may help

Poison Oak

as a last resort in case you cannot count to three, or in the event that you play fast and loose with the three-leaved creeper "because it never bothered me before." That old favorite, Calamine lotion, is still a blessed relief from all that itching, painful dermatitis, just as it was in Grandma's day.

Normal, unbroken leaves and stems of the pernicious plant are seldom harmful, by the way. Perhaps that's the reason you didn't get poison ivy the first time although you're not so lucky now. It's that resinous sap that does the damage. When the plant is rubbed or bruised the sap begins to flow—and in a few hours you begin to itch.

Incidentally, hot steaming compresses give me the most relief of any treatment I have tried. Or, on a hot July night, try rubbing the affected parts with an ice cube. And don't worry that you'll spread the inflammation further by rubbing, scratching or sponging. The fluid from broken blisters is noninfectious. It's merely your tender hide's reaction to an allergy.

The time-honored practice of scrubbing with yellow soap and water after contact with poison ivy will lessen your problems. It probably will not let you off scot-free, as your reaction apparently began when you and that persnickety plant rubbed elbows, so to speak. However, the treatment removes any dried sap lurking on your skin or hair, ready to cause further woes.

If you went out and gingerly snipped the plant off during its dormant period (when the danger is lessened), better wash those clippers. And if you have waded through the stuff, dump your clothes into hot soapy water, too. Such inanimate objects can serve as carriers.

Animals can serve as carriers, too. Poison ivy doesn't

seem to bother them, but they generously share it with you after they've rolled or played in it.

All the invective you've hurled at poison ivy and poison oak can be repeated, chapter and verse, for poison sumac. In fact, you can double it: contact with this plant may put you in the hospital. Luckily you'll not meet it unless you're a bog-trotter or swamp-walker, for it grows with wet feet. Thus it helpfully fills in the places where poison ivy is absent.

Sumacs in general have compound leaves, with five to eleven leaflets—sometimes more. The leaflets of the harmless species usually have sawtoothed edges. In these friendly forms the twigs are often covered with a coating of hair. One common species has the hair so dense that it's like the "velvet" on the antlers of a deer. Appropriately enough, it's known as staghorn sumac. You'll see its fuzzy clusters of red berries at the ends of those unshorn branches in almost any overgrown pasture. In autumn its foliage turns old roadbanks and fencerows to a bright scarlet.

The leaves of poison sumac will color up in autumn, too, but its berries are yellow-white and form bunches that droop from the stem instead of standing smartly at the tip. There are no sawtoothed edges on the leaflets, either. The twigs are clean-shaven with few of the cozy whiskers of the more hospitable types. Perhaps this smoothness, coupled with an almost varnished redness on the central axis of the compound leaf, is responsible for poison sumac's scientific name: *Toxicodendron vernix*, "the poison plant that's varnished."

You may find poison sumac in swamps anywhere east of the Mississippi and up into Canada. And while you're

Poison Sumac

looking for trouble, search for a couple of other renegades: poison parsnip, for instance, or water hemlock. A few persons get a mild dermatitis from touching these plants, too, although the chief danger is in eating them. Their general appearance is enough like carrots or parsnips so that people may make a serious mistake and take them home for dinner.

Even more serious may be your misidentification of a dry-ground relative, the poison hemlock. It was a tea made from the leaves of poison hemlock, forced upon the beloved Socrates, that cut short the great teacher's career in 399 B.C.

These plants, by the way, are no relation to the benign and graceful true hemlock tree, *Tsuga canadensis*. Rather, they are members of the carrot family. It seems impossible that our tasty garden carrots, parsnips, anise, dill and caraway could have such rascally relatives, but then, that's often the way with families.

Most of these plants, good or bad, bear the family likeness: one or more carrotlike roots, finely divided foliage and tiny flowers that look as if they're borne at the points of the ribs of an inverted umbrella.

This special flower arrangement, or umbel, gives the whole group its name: *Umbelliferae*, the umbrella-bearers. Go into any field or garden and you may find a few for yourself: wild carrot or Queen Anne's lace; wild celery; fool's parsley. They're all look-alikes for their cultivated kinfolk. In fact, let a carrot stay in the garden beyond its normal first year, and it will put out an impressive stalk the second season—umbel and all.

Better not try to separate the sheep from the goats in this freewheeling flock. You could be betting your life on your decision—literally. A few mouthfuls of the wrong

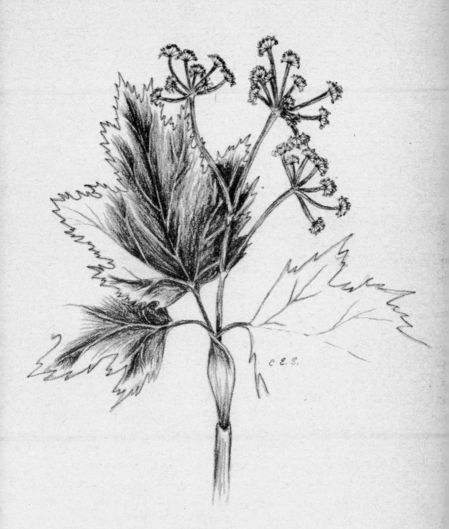

Poison Parsnip or Cow Parsnip

root, leaf or stem may bring on nausea and convulsions. A good helping can give you a terminal case of indigestion.

So, if you spot the carrotlike foliage, the fleshy taproot, those inverted-umbrella flowers, better let well enough alone. They may be fine for table decorations, but please don't eat the centerpiece.

Actually there are hundreds of confusing look-alikes in the plant world. No single person could spot them all. Even if you're armed with a good book on plant identification, you may still be in the woods, so to speak. You find such willy-nilly—but straight-faced—phrases as "flowers growing at the tip of stem except when borne elsewhere," and "twigs smooth unless hairs or thorns are present." Or, as my botany professor, G. Safford Torrey, said in a fit of exasperation, "*e pluribus*—except when *unum*!"

The trouble, of course, is that plants are living things. They just don't fit handily into somebody's written description. Nor does any living bit of creation, for that matter. You can describe a human being in general terms, yes. But can you draw a word picture of dear Aunt Tessie so I'd recognize her in a crowd? I doubt it.

The best thing, short of abandoning you to the mercies of all the impostors and pretenders in the plant world—or lapsing into a thousand-page encyclopedia right now—is to pass along a few hints that may help you in most encounters with plants.

One way you can load the scales in your favor is just to refuse to have anything to do with the things. Except, of course, the plants you grow, or buy in the food store, or whose fibers you use as clothing, or whose tissues supply your home and your tennis racket and your wedge heels, or whose oxygen you breathe, or whose extracts flavor your cakes, color your hair, calm your nerves, speed up your

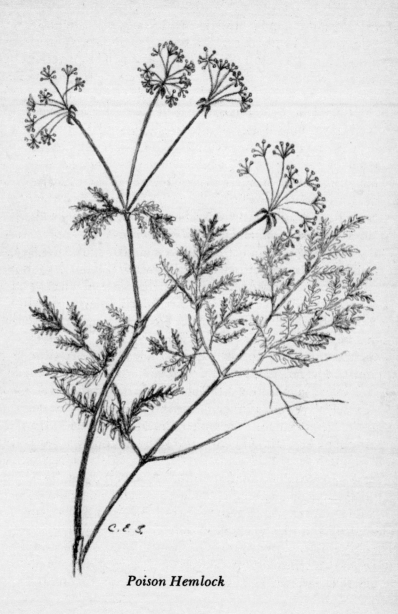

C.E.S.

Poison Hemlock

heart, slow it down—but you get the idea. You can't turn your back on plants.

If you're interested in the delightful world of edible plants, get hold of a book or two that helps you recognize them. You can have lots of fun with a few familiar kinds —dandelions, for instance, or wild strawberries or hickory nuts. It's pretty difficult to make serious mistakes if you stick to such relatively foolproof species.

A quicker way, and often more fun, is to find someone who's interested in edible plants. Then the two of you can go wild-grocery shopping together. Such an arrangement has a further advantage in case you end up with the wrong food: you've got somebody to blame.

So reluctantly, I must leave you and your taste buds to the gourmets and gurus who ply you with books, pamphlets, radio and TV ads on the newly enfranchised but ancient craft of living off the land. Such relinquishment saddens me, as wild foods have been favorites of mine since those days long ago when our whole family made its annual pilgrimage to the swamp to get a mess of yellow cowslips or marsh marigolds, *Caltha palustris*.

In the hands-off department, however, there are a few more words that could yet be spoken. Most of the time, of course, you can spot the briars and brambles before you blunder into them—barring such refinements as the deceptively soft hairs on certain cactuses that cover the hidden needles. Although the southern and western realm of the cactus is quite well out of the scope of this book, there is one group of irritant plants that we should touch on— figuratively, that is. These are the nettles.

There are a number of kinds of nettles in our woods and fields. One kind grows in almost a pure stand at the edges of the Long Trail through our Green Mountains of

Stinging Nettle

Vermont. It must leave a memorable impression on lightly clad summer hikers in shorts and sneakers. Another species of nettle made a good barrier around my garden when I lived on Long Island. I didn't mind sharing my crops with the neighborhood youngsters, but the garden happened to be on a shortcut to the local ballfield—until the nettles moved in all by themselves and changed things.

It's Going to Sting Me!

Nettles are herbaceous plants; that is, they have no persistent woody stem, but come up anew each spring. They may be a foot high or taller than your head, depending on the species. Nettle leaves are elliptical, with saw-toothed edges, looking somewhat like the leaves of their tall first cousin, the elm. The plants have small greenish flowers that often hang in stringlike clusters near the axils where the leaves join the stem.

Look closely at a nettle and you'll see that it bears a number of hairs and bristles. Some of these hairs are like those in other plants: downy or stiff or somewhere in between, but quite harmless. Other hairs, however, are quite different. These hairs are hollow and filled with an irritant fluid related to oxalic acid.

The points of the stinging hairs are as brittle as glass. They are often tipped with a tiny, fragile bulb. When you brush against the plant the bulb shatters, leaving a jagged, splintery needle. The needle instantly penetrates the flesh —and you have just met a nettle.

Luckily, the sting from most nettles soon dies away. For half an hour or more, however, your sensations run the gamut from fiery burning to intense itching. Calamine lotion helps here, or try a simple wet pack of baking soda or just plain mud. You can also rub that tender welt with the juice of the touch-me-not plant—which treatment, by the way, is often good for poison ivy rash.

Touch-me-not is also known as jewelweed or snapweed. You may see its herbaceous growth, sometimes shoulder-high, around old buildings and roadsides. Thus it's apt to be found in close company with the nettles. The oval leaves and slender stems are watery in appearance, almost translucent. The common touch-me-not has orange flowers spotted with brown and shaped like a little dunce cap.

They are garnished with a spur that hangs forward from the bottom.

Woodland touch-me-not is similar, but with pale yellow flowers. It often grows, most helpfully, in patches right near the forest nettles. The common name comes from the sudden bursting of the swollen seedpods when touched, throwing the seeds several yards away. The name is carried over into botany too: *Impatiens*, "the hasty one."

Incidentally, the nettles are also well named. Most of them bear the generic title *Urtica*, which derives from the Latin *ūro*, which gives all the warning that's needed: "I burn." The woodland nettle, *Laportea*, is named after the nineteenth-century entomologist, Count Francois L. de Laporte—who, conceivably, might have had mixed feelings about lending his name to an itchy, pestiferous druid.

One more point about nettles. Although I've had little to say about edible plants, here is an exception. Once you have discovered the fiery plant, you can yet put it to good use. It makes a fine edible green, impossible as that may seem. Put on your leather gloves and pick a few nettles. Cover them with water and bring to a boil. That hot water wilts those brittle hairs and flushes away their juice.

Drain the water carefully, add butter and salt, and you've got a great-tasting dish. Peg and I serve nettles to our guests every summer. At first we rechristened them as wild spinach, but after a number of years with outdoor foods we no longer bother. Our guests are suspicious, anyway.

Other prickly plants can add something extra to a leisurely stroll. They may range from hawthorns with four-inch spikes to the common mullein (*Verbascum*), whose great, plushy leaves look as if they're made of flannel. The fuzz on the leaves is brittle and tends to rub off. If those tiny hairs get on some of your more tender portions, they may itch for the rest of the day.

Between such extremes can be found a whole gamut of greenery, actually presenting more of a nuisance than a threat. Among these troublemakers are plants with such intriguing titles as burdock, sticktights and devil's pitch-forks. Add to these a catclaw bush and a wait-a-minute, plus saw grass, tearthumb, and smartweed, and you have quite an assemblage lying in ambush.

There are plenty more than these, of course. And you really cannot blame the plants for giving you a tough time. Wherever there are plants they may be animals all poised to: (1) chew on them, (2) walk on them or (3) nest in them. Such behavior is hard on the plants. Even worse, the plant has to sit there and take it unless it comes up with some form of protection. Hence, the spikes of the hawthorn, the hooks of catclaw and wait-a-minute, and the sawteeth of tearthumb and smartweed.

Then, since nature is no slouch about making use of resources at hand, the animals are also pressed into service to help those plants get around. Spherical burrs help the seeds of burdock (*Arctium*) find greener pastures, for instance, as do the flat, adhesive pods of the sticktight (*Desmodium*). Then there are those little black gaffs of the beggar's-ticks or devil's pitchforks whose scientific name aptly describes their twin-pronged appearance: *Bidens*, "two toothed."

Along with scores of other kinds of burrs and stickers, these prickly seeds may hitch a ride on almost any passerby, human or otherwise. Discovered some time later, they are pulled off, combed out and tossed away—usually right out in the open, a few moments after they're discovered. The erstwhile host, glad to be rid of them, thus helps to compound his own misery by scattering the seeds in new and better fields.

The same idea is wrapped up in edible fruits and nuts, of course. Here, the edible portion is often expendable; the plant wastes it, so to speak, so that the seeds might be carried along and discarded at the end of the meal. Peg and I have found many an apple tree in the forest—souvenir of an earlier day when some wanderer tossed an apple core aside. We also find lone nut trees in odd situations where some squirrel carefully buried its treasure and then absentmindedly left it to fate.

In the berries and other small edibles with hard pits or seeds, the whole fruit may be eaten at a gulp. The soft parts are digested, but the pits resist the internal flood of enzymes. Their hard shells allow them to tumble along, unaffected, until they are finally eliminated from the body. Many are deserted over rocks or sandbanks or water, but some are deposited on good soil—and given an added pat on the back by the little mound of fertilizer voided at the same time.

In separating the good from the bad, an animal often relies on its natural instincts—plus the example set by others of its kind. We humans are usually denied such advantages. In fact, we're often denied even the chance to be human, what with clothing that shapes us, cosmetics that color us and chemicals that deodorize us. Thus any urgings, if we *did* have them, would soon be stifled.

This, of course, is where the many good books on wild plants come in. By separating friend from foe among the leafy inhabitants of our countryside, the books help to pick up where instinct has long since left off. I have seventeen such books on my shelves, plus dozens of booklets and pamphlets purporting to serve as faithful guides for any situation. To digest their information here, so to speak, would be more of a task than you or I would care to undertake.

So, in a word, if you're interested in the great, natural supermarket of edibles spread out across our continent, there are many "shopping guides" already written to help you along. And if your interest is merely to maintain a whole skin and well-balanced innards following your sojourn into the wilds of a city park or the perils of the northwoods, your best policy is, generally speaking, hands off. You'll miss many a good meal, but you may save yourself a mountain of grief, too.

That also goes for another whole world of plant life: the arresting creations known as mushrooms. Walking through the woods or fields, you may come across these intriguing fungi almost any time of the year.

Mushrooms grow on the sides of trees, or in undisturbed soil, on old compost heaps—even on golf courses. They grow singly, in clusters, or in attractive "fairy rings" of dozens of individuals scattered around a circle several feet in diameter. They're crimson, brown, yellow, white or almost any other color you wish to name. One "bleeds" a convincing red when it's cut; another exudes a milky juice. Some smell great and taste terrible; others go down like honey—and come right up again.

My mushroom books describe over a hundred species that can be found in our eastern section of the continent. Some list the "toadstools"—poisonous or unwholesome kinds—separately from the edible mushrooms, while most of them are content to make pronouncements on the edibility of each species as they come to it.

Then, too, I find something slightly disquieting in the authorship of one of these books: the book was begun by a gentleman who described the taste of dozens of species—until, suddenly, the rest of the book is finished by someone else. No word of what happened to the original author.

The trouble with mushrooms is that you cannot lay down a law that will fit them all. An old "proof" of a poisonous kind is to dunk a silver spoon into the pot while they're cooking; if the spoon tarnishes, you toss out the mushrooms—and then, I suppose, you decide how to rejuvenate the spoon. However, there are certain mushrooms that produce alarming effects on your interior although they're not noticed in the least by the spoon. Besides, even if "tarnish" equals "tainted," a perfectly good egg will do a fine discoloration job on the best silver spoon you've got.

You cannot even tell good from bad by taste or texture. *Amanita muscaria* and *Amanita phalloides*—the fly mushroom and the death angel—both responsible for many deaths, are delicious to taste. Or so I'm told; I've never had the pleasure myself. On the other hand, a certain species of oyster mushroom is as tough as a piece of cold liver, but well worth the muscle power in getting it beyond the knife-and-fork stage.

No; I must admit I've never found a single way to pick out all good mushrooms from all bad. With perhaps a couple dozen species bidding for your attention on a woodland walk on any particular day, there are bound to be exceptions to any rule

And now, as I think of it further, even *this* rule has an exception. As far as I have ever been able to tell in sampling mushrooms for three decades and talking in tones of suitable gravity with other naturalists, you cannot go wrong if your foray into the world of the mycophagist (mushroom-eater) involves an adventure with the giant puffball.

Puffballs, it seems, vary in size, flavor and plain good taste. A few of them are tough as a shirt collar and some of them may have a decided laxative effect if eaten when overripe. None, however, is downright poisonous. And as long as you stick to the huge *Lycoperdon giganteum*, which looks like something left over from somebody's basketball game, you're on solid ground. Few things in nature— except an outsized bleached grapefruit, perhaps, resemble a giant puffball.

The great spherical mushroom begins life as a tiny spore that grows into a maze of threads (mycelium) permeating the soil. Once annually, usually in August or September, the threads send forth a nubbin that penetrates the roof of the topsoil and appears aboveground as a tiny white marble. The nourishment from the mycelium pours steadily into the nubbin, causing it to swell hour after hour. You cannot actually watch it grow as you lie there on your stomach in the grass of the lawn or pasture, but if you look at it two or three times a day you'll note a steady increase in size. Overnight, for instance, it may grow from the girth of a golf ball to that of a baseball.

During several exuberant days the puffball takes on astounding dimensions. The largest I have actually weighed tipped the scales at thirteen pounds, and I've seen a number that were larger.

There'll be no other mushroom that you could logically mistake for a giant puffball in full glory. However, many mushrooms begin their careers aboveground as "buttons" that appear much like tiny spheres. To tell a button from a true puffball, watch it for a day or so. If it continues to grow with no differentiation into stem and cap, you're in luck. Then, to be certain—and when you're ready for your gourmet meal—slice it right down through the middle.

If the whole affair is mealy, snowy white and homogeneous throughout, get out the skillet. Remove the leathery outer skin and lower a couple of half-inch slabs into a little sizzling butter. Cook until nicely browned—and you'll wonder, as I have, why you ever kicked puffballs around when you were a kid.

One slight suggestion. As soon as the puffball is mature, its immaculate interior rapidly turns yellow, and then brown as its spores develop. If it's anything but purest white inside, don't eat it. It'll be gooey and somewhat laxative. Give it a kick, yourself, if you want—or better, wait until it has changed completely to its millions of powdery spores and *then* thrash the life out of it. In this way you'll help to populate the countryside with delicious puffballs.

As for the hundred or so other species of mushrooms you may find in our eastern woods and pastures, there are excellent field guides that will identify nearly every one. And the old warning is as good for mushrooms as it was for the rest of the cast of characters in this chapter: if you do not know what it is, let it be.

But with puffballs—ah, that's another matter. Peg and I always fry up a few spare slices in the fall and put them in the freezer. They are there now, in fact—just awaiting the opening of that freezer door and the friendly nod that says we're about to have a hearty dinner.

So, if you happen to be in the neighborhood, we'd like to invite you in for steak and mushrooms. Let us know you're coming so we can exhume the proper amount of puffballs from the freezer.

Depending, of course, on how large a steak you bring.

10·...And Sounds That Go Bump in the Night

When my brother and sister and I were young, we spent almost every summer night sleeping outdoors. There were two reasons for our juvenile version of roughing it: (1) it was fun, and (2) it was about twenty degrees cooler than the upstairs bedrooms of our century-old farmhouse.

We slept in our old army tent with its ridgepole, stakes and supporting ropes. We needed the tent even on clear nights, as the cold New England air almost always brought a drenching dew.

Every few days we'd relocate for a change of scene: from the backyard to the pasture, say, or to the pine grove or the bank of the brook. In the process, Irma and Jim and I spent nearly as many hours awake as asleep in the tent; lying wide-eyed in the dark and deciphering the squeaks and thumps, buzzes and wails that surrounded our baggy boudoir.

I remember, for instance, the thundering hoofs that grew so loud that we leaped up in alarm just as the tent collapsed. Old Daisy, our normally placid Guernsey cow, had become startled at something and ran full tilt into the tent ropes. Doubtless she doubled her speed when the canvas attacked her, too—although we were too busy with our own troubles to notice.

Then there was the night we camped out in what was apparently the domain of a screech owl. The pigeon-sized bird divided its time among several trees and the peak of the tent, waiting until we were almost asleep and then serenading us. First it called from the limbs of an old butternut, then from a sugar maple, then from the ridgepole, six feet above our heads. The little owl's call is not a screech at all, but a quavering, descending cry. To us it's one of the most melodious sounds in nature.

A number of owls, in fact, have a pleasant-sounding call —unless you're a mouse or a rabbit or a bird perched in a tree. From a few hundred feet away the great horned and barred owls sound like the barking of a distant dog. The horned owl calls in a phrase of four or five hoots, while the barred owl's cry is in two groups of four, causing it to be called the "eight-hooter." Its sound is often interpreted as "Who cooks for you? Who cooks for you-all?" with a slur on the last syllable.

During late winter and early spring when their families are getting started, these large owls may utter an unearthly scream. You'd never attribute such noise to a bird: it sounds more like the start of a cat fight. Luckily, by the time your summer vacation comes around and you head for the outdoors, the owls are back to more normal utterances.

The barred, screech and horned owls are the common species of our northeastern states and adjacent Canada. Less frequently you may hear the gutteral cry of the barn owl around old buildings, sounding like two or three disjointed snores up there under the eaves. If you're really lucky you might be serenaded by one of the world's smallest owls: the saw-whet, whose tinkertoy voice matches its tiny dimensions.

The call of this robin-sized owl is a single high note, repeated about twice a second, sometimes for more than a minute. One evening a woman called me on the phone. "There's a strange gadget in the woods behind the house," she said. "None of us has heard anything like it before."

In answer to my request as to exactly how it sounded, there was a pause at the other end of the phone. Then I heard a window being opened. "Here," she said, "listen for yourself."

She held the receiver out the window. Through miles of wire and switchboards, and up over the spine of the Green Mountains came the unmistakable call of the saw-whet: *toot-toot-toot-toot* . . . on and on. It did, indeed, sound as if someone were filing the teeth of a saw, one by one, with short strokes; hence the little bird's common name.

When I told her the identity of the sound, she was both relieved and disappointed. "My husband thought it might be some sort of weather balloon that had come to earth," she said. "And the kids had it all tabbed for a flying saucer."

That's the way with noises in the night: they can fool you. The sound made by many a bird or animal would scarcely be noticed in the hubbub of day, but at night it is presented against a backdrop of gloom and mystery. Under such circumstances your imagination can conjure up all sorts of things.

One time, for instance, my grandmother was helping my

father in repapering the walls of my bedroom. Plaster and old paper were all over the floor as I gingerly tiptoed through the debris, turned out the light, and climbed into bed. No sooner had I settled down, however, than there was an intermittent hissing, almost like something breathing there in the dark.

Sitting bolt upright, I tried to figure out an explanation. But as it continued, *f-f-f-t . . . f-f-f-t*, my figuring ability remained at zero. Hastily I reached over and turned on the light.

Clambering through the mess was a little dark beetle the size of a jellybean. Attracted by the light, it had flown into the room and had fallen to the floor. There it soon became covered with plaster dust. Running about in confusion, the poor creature hurried around and under and across those pieces of paper. The loose material acted as a sounding board, and there was my scary visitor—down on its luck, with things getting worse.

I picked the beetle up, dusted it off, and tossed it out the window Probably it was lucky that it had become plastered at night, for the daytime noises would have hidden the sounds of its struggle.

Take the sounds of other creatures that may share your abode, as well: the rodents, for instance. As you recall, the front teeth of these little creatures never stop growing, so they must be forever gnawing, gnawing just to keep them worn down. And since your house, with its intriguing smells and nice hollow walls seems to issue a standing invitation, as it were, the rodents are quick to accept. There, among the tasty two-by-fours, the savory studs and all the other pleasant paraphernalia that can be found in a house, the bucktoothed rodent finds plenty to keep those incisors whetted and sharp.

The spaces within the walls magnify the sound of scampering and the noise of gnawing until you're ready to move out and let the mice have the place. That drafty old farmhouse of ours was not insulated in the exterior walls, and as the whatever-they-weres traveled over the lath and plaster they'd loosen bits of the plaster, sending it rattling down to floor level. Occasionally one would venture forth into Mother's pantry. Then, as it nibbled on a cereal box or other tempting item, the sound of its feasting could be heard all over the house.

We tried to keep the numbers of these little freeloaders down to a minimum, of course. With a barn close by, however, there was always a new source of supply. One of Dad's frequent activities was to spread slices of bread with peanut butter and phosphorus paste while we stood around and solemnly surveyed the creation of that lethal meal. Then we'd watch as he cut the bread into cubes. Down cellar he would go, followed by his three silent offspring. We knew, as he carefully placed the poison, that the companionable sound of rats and mice in the walls would cease for a few weeks—until new pioneers ventured in from the fields or the barn.

Rodents or not, a house can be rich with nighttime sound. Peg and I were overnight visitors in a venerable home near Toronto. We were guests of Al and Josie Boudreau, their cat, their dog—and their deathwatch beetle. The beetle lived in the woodwork of an antique bureau that stood by our bed. Several times before we'd drop off to sleep each night, we'd listen to the ticking of a "watch" coming from somewhere in the innards of that bureau—even though there seemed to be nothing in any of the drawers.

Deathwatches are actually the grubs, or larvae, of a

beetle about the size of a small grain of corn. The larva drills through well-aged wood, helping to create those wormholes that make the wood so valuable. Occasionally, for reasons apparent only to its obscure little psyche, the larva pauses in its woodworking chores and taps its hard little jaws against the side of its burrow. Perhaps it's a message to other beetle larvae: "This is my Louis Quinze chiffonier—go find your own furniture." Or, more likely, it's merely an expression of nervous activity, sort of like twiddling your thumbs or tapping with a pencil.

Probably such behavior is more common than we realize, but most of the time we cannot hear it. In the stillness of a sleeping house, however, and magnified in the cavernous interior of the right piece of furniture or a reverberating wall, the deathwatch is a flawless—if ghostly—timepiece.

Such an eerie accompaniment to someone's lonely vigil by a sick bed has long been thought to be a sign of impending doom. The little grub, however, is innocent of such intentions as it goes on with its odd little antics: *tick-tick-tick-tick*, for half a minute at a time.

Our tiny unseen roommate performed at will, without any apparent urging on our part. Its country cousins in their old logs and stumps may also pause in their excavations to tap out a little message of their own. The ticking of such a disembodied clock on a summer's evening may make you wonder if you've been in the woods too long.

Sometimes you can trigger a suitable reaction merely by thumping a likely log. I remember stopping at a pile of well-weathered pulpwood with a forester in Maryland; he gave the pile a whack with his axe and started a veritable clockworks. The woodpile still sounded like castanets when we sauntered away several minutes later; apparently the agitated little borers kept each other going.

Just as you'd probably never suspect an insect of imitating a timepiece, so you'd never guess the origin of a host of other unusual noises. Unusual from our standpoint, that is, although they are quite normal to the creatures that make them. If you've ever been near a marsh on a spring evening when the American bittern tuned up with his slow, measured stake-driver call, you might be tempted to take bets that it was somebody pounding a fencepost. In reality it's the love song of this brown-striped, short-legged heron: um-*ker*-chug! um-*ker*-chug! um-*ker*-chug!

The sound of your first bullfrog will doubtless prove a revelation, too. Long esteemed as the source of fried frogs legs, old "jug-o-rum" makes a deep, sonorous noise that sounds like his nickname. A friend of mine asked a gentleman from Africa to guess what kind of critter was bellowing in the pond behind their house one evening. The Afrikander, used to such noises as the "whump" of a hippopotamus and the roar of the great cats, decided it was some kind of large mammal, or perhaps an alligator. He was quite surprised—in fact, incredulous—when he was told it was only a frog. Indeed, when he left several days later he still didn't believe it.

"Come on, now," he said, just as he departed. "What kind of creature do you *really* have out there in your lake?"

You may be the startled recipient of other noises from the water, as well. The slap of a beaver's tail, delivered as an alarm signal, can be heard across a lake for more than a mile. As you drift in your canoe, or slowly make your way along the shore of a beaver pond some evening, the resounding crash of that flattened tail will stay with you long after the ripples have died away.

For sheer wildness in sound try the laughter of a loon. Many vacationers and campers refer to the bird's cry as like that of a maniac; indeed, the words "loon" and "lunatic" have a common beginning. Both hearken back to *Luna*, the moon, who is supposed to shatter the mind of man and beast at certain times of the month. And, if you don't know what to expect, the sudden outburst of a loon, rising and falling like insane laughter out on the lake, may well put an end to your night's sleep, right there.

Personally, I find great joy in the call of the loon. Riding out there in the evening mists, its back awash and its lance-like beak pointed skyward as it sends its ringing cry, the bird is the essence of wildness to many as it pauses in its yearly rounds from Central America to the chilly sub-arctic. You can see it diving after fish on wintering grounds in our southern states, but to hear its mirthless yodel in breeding season you have to visit more northerly lakes. And I wouldn't blame you if you took a tranquilizer along. After the "helldiver" has laughed at you on a lonesome lake, you may feel that you need it.

Incidentally, the lake may turn an auditory trick all by itself. Along the shore of Grand Lake in New Brunswick, there's a wave-worn rock that has been hollowed into a cave. During periods when the water is at the right level that cave sighs and moans as the breakers slosh around in its depths. Thunder Hole, at Acadia National Park in Maine, grumbles and complains almost constantly. Then, when an outsized breaker piles into its narrow entrance, it imprisons the air which suddenly erupts, spraying scurrying vacationists with salt water.

There are thousands of such blowholes along shores all over the world. Some are visited constantly by tourists, while others will become apparent only to you as they mutter and mumble after you've settled down in your lakeside retreat.

... And Sounds That Go Bump in the Night

Peg and I stood and looked into one of the most famous blowholes of all: the black pit in Hawaiian lava where, legend says, the Lizard God is imprisoned forever. Although the pit has an opening scarce the size of a barrel, it connects with a vast underground labyrinth extending into the boiling surf. As the breakers crash into the labyrinth a hundred yards away, there's a sharp intake and exhalation at the pit—the Lizard God in sudden pain. Wave piles on wave into the honeycombed lava, and spray shoots high out of the opening as the god thrashes around one more futile time.

Then, too, there's Flushaway Falls. Each winter, as the ice forms on a little brook near my house, only the swiftest water remains uncovered. Then, following a couple of those crystal nights when the air is so cold that your breath freezes in tiny ephemeral needles on your lips, the final cascade receives its icy roof. Except for a few sheltered air holes the brook is covered at last.

The water continues its course, even though its sound is muffled. As it goes over a certain rocky ledge you can see the tracery of great bubbles on the underside of the clear ice. They look like enormous, silvery amoebas. About every two minutes the bubbles begin to combine into one great pocket of air. In a short time they have collected into a space as large as a card table and several inches deep. Finally, able to maintain itself no longer, the huge pocket escapes out through a half-hidden air hole at the far side. The sound, as it rushes away and is replaced by new water, is precisely like our familiar bathroom fixture.

As ponds and lakes freeze deeper, the thickening ice is placed under enormous stress. Even though there is no open water to produce waves, the frozen surface responds to the force of a steady wind. As the wind continues it drags on the ice, trying to pile it up on one shore while pulling away from the other. In addition, rising or falling water level may cause the ice to shift, as may changes in temperature. The result of all this strain is seen—and heard—as "seasoners" or "weather cracks." These are sudden splits that race across the ice from one shore to another faster than your eye can follow.

Weather cracks sing, groan, or sound like rifle shots. If you happen to be standing out on the great expanse of Lake Champlain, as I have, when one of those fractures appears beneath you, it could be downright upsetting—if it didn't take place before you had time to comprehend it. Grace and Irv Kolbas, who have an apartment house in St. Albans Bay north of Burlington, regularly have to assure jittery tenants that those strange sounds are not intruders but "seasoners" hurtling across the darkened ice.

Usually the weather cracks heal themselves. Occasionally, especially in late winter, they occur in several directions at once, breaking the ice into chunks of various sizes. Two ice fishermen on Lake Champlain went out for one last fishing trip of the season on a blustery day. The wind was fierce, however, so they headed back for shore. They were almost on land when several cracks rent the ice around them. They found themselves on a floe about the size of a tennis court, with a thin line of water welling up all around its edge.

Then they felt a gentle rocking. The whole surface of the lake was breaking. The floe cracked down the middle and the line of water between them and the shore rapidly became wider. The gale was driving them out into the lake.

There was no choice. Plunging into the black water,

they swam across its width and managed to scramble up onto the ice beyond. From there they raced to shore. Exhausted and nearly frozen, they collapsed in the arms of several people who ran to meet them. Luckily, a house and warm bath were close by, and tragedy was averted.

The woods, as well as the waters, give voice to the chill of winter. On coldest nights the silence of the forest may be punctuated at any moment by a sound like a gunshot as some treetrunk cracks with the frost. That old maple on your lawn may complain just as loudly too, and even the timbers of your house groan and creak. Their sudden sound, in the stillness of the night, may make you think you're being invaded.

If the wind blows, countless knotholes, twigs and pine needles turn into whistles. Tree branches rub against each other until the whole forest seems peopled with ghosts. Two yellow birch limbs in the woods behind my house squeak gently when there's a breeze from the north. As the wind rises they chirp like crickets. When it's blowing a gale the tree pulls out all the stops. There up in the forest, it sounds as if someone is stepping on a cat.

Smaller sounds that would be overlooked in daytime take on alarming proportions at night. A whitefooted mouse, drumming its front feet in agitation, becomes of great significance when the tiny tattoo is rattled out on a dry leaf or piece of bark. In the daytime you wouldn't even hear it. Nor would you hear the faint canary-like trill of the mouse as it protests your presence in a series of rapid-fire squeaks.

You'd scarcely hear the hind feet of a rabbit, either, as it thumped out a warning that you were trespassing on its domain. At night, however, that thumping is matched by the pounding of your heart as the unfamiliar sound suddenly throbs through the night.

I've heard the scream of a wildcat two or three times, and the grunt of a bear twice in the woods that surround our home. The falsetto wails and complaints of a lovelorn pair of porcupines have accompanied us on many an evening walk in autumn. But the most chilling sound I have heard was one that shattered the air of a May evening in a Connecticut swamp.

I was a zoology student at the time. My special interest was aquatic biology, and I wanted to catch a few frogs for a large terrarium in the laboratory. Armed with a flashlight and clad in a pair of boots, I stealthily approached a pool where spring peepers, leopard frogs and American toads were mating, singing and kicking up a ruckus in the water.

My collecting efforts were rewarded, and several of the goggle-eyed amphibians soon swam in the large jar I carried. I had been bent over for half an hour, absorbed in my work, and straightened up to give my back a rest.

As I stood upright, there was an explosion in the water a few yards away. A splintering sound announced that some great animal had run into a bush. At the same instant I was paralyzed by a snorting scream.

I was unable to move. Then there was the noise of splashing as the animal ran off into the night. Coming to my senses, I turned the flashlight in the direction it had taken, but saw nothing

After my heart had stopped pounding and my knees felt strong enough to walk again, I waded over toward that broken bush. It was easy enough to determine the cause of the commotion; several identifying hairs had caught in the twigs as the animal made its escape. Apparently unaware of my presence, it had wandered close—until I stood up and frightened it. The perpetrator of that terrifying snort had been none other than the gentle, graceful whitetailed deer.

Since then I have heard the snort of a deer several times. It always startles me, but never so much as on that peaceful night among the frogs. Luckily, my boots were hitched to my belt; otherwise I might have jumped right out of them.

One last event. It took place at the home of Betsy Schenk, whose drawings grace the pages of this book. Betsy and Bill live on a country road, in much the same rural Vermont surroundings as mine. One night Betsy woke Bill, hastily cautioning him to be quiet.

"SH-h-h!" she whispered. "Someone's on the back porch."

They could hear stealthy footsteps. Then there was a muffled cough.

Bill got up and groped in the dark for a weapon. Then, covertly dialing the telephone, he called the police.

While waiting for the Law, he tried to get a look at the intruder. The night was pitch dark, however, and he could see little. Finally, unable to stand the suspense any longer, he yanked open the door.

There stood his burglar—the neighbor's horse. Finding a break in the fence, the horse had wandered into his yard. Several planks were on the ground near the porch; the horse must have stepped on one or two, thus creating the "footsteps." The muffled cough, doubtless, had been little more than a sigh as the animal grazed peacefully on the Schenks' back lawn.

Grabbing the phone, Bill hastily canceled the midnight alarm. Luckily, a radio dispatch was able to head the prowl car off, and they were spared a face-to-face explanation.

"The police were amused by it all," Betsy told me, "—or at least they said they were. The next time we give them a call, we're going to check all the neighbor's livestock first."

Her remark, perhaps, could serve as a wrap-up for this whole book. Most of the sounds that go bump in the night have an explanation that would seem obvious by daylight. In the same way, there's a good reason for the behavior of those threatening critters that seem forever poised for a blistering attack on you and me. A little time spent in becoming familiar with them may increase your respect, and even your admiration, for the whole company of them.

Indeed, there may be a further reward of such high-principled research: you just might deepen your understanding of the loudest, lumpiest, most threatening Unknown of them all—*Homo sapiens*, the critter who writes and reads books.

Index

[Page numbers in *italics* refer to illustrations.]

Index

Index

Index

Catalog

If you are interested in a list of fine Paperback
books, covering a wide range of subjects
and interests, send your name and address,
requesting your free catalog, to:

McGraw-Hill Paperbacks
1221 Avenue of Americas
New York, N.Y. 10020